Praise for
The Truth About Making Smart Decisions

"*The Truth About Making Smart Decisions* offers a truly valuable and entertaining journey through the complex terrain of decision making. Robert Gunther combines a writer's gift of the pen with a keen understanding of human nature, drawing upon his own experiences, business anecdotes, and vignettes from other walks of life. His selection of traps, insights, and truths are edifying as well as amusing, and many readers will recognize themselves as he exposes our weaknesses, and occasional brilliance, as we carve the trajectory of our life one decision after the next."

Paul J. H. Schoemaker, Ph.D.,
coauthor of *Decision Traps and Winning Decisions*

"Robert Gunther crystallizes years of expertise and insight in business writing into a book on probably life's most important matter: decision making. How do you do it and how do you do it *much* better? He offers many tools to organize the mind and maximize your ability to be a leader and money maker."

Rick Rickertsen, Managing Partner of Pine Creek Partners and
author of *The Buyout Book* and *Sell Your Business Your Way*

"We make decision errors predictably, and Robert Gunther offers fifty ways of taking decisions more intelligently. *The Truth About Making Smart Decisions* is a concise and actionable guide for what to consider when facing critical choice points."

Michael Useem, Ph.D., Wharton Professor of Management and
author of *The Go Point: When It's Time to Decide*

"If you think decision making is cut and dried, this book will make you think again. In *The Truth About Making Smart Decisions*, Robert Gunther offers challenging insights on how factors from sleep to intuition to emotions to mental models affect the quality of our decisions. He urges readers to take a broader view and raises issues that anyone should consider in making smarter decisions."

Yoram (Jerry) Wind, Ph.D., The Lauder Professor and Wharton Professor of Marketing,
and coauthor of *The Power of Impossible Thinking*

THE TRUTH ABOUT

MAKING SMART DECISIONS

Robert E. Gunther

© 2008 by Pearson Education, Inc.

Publishing as FT Press

Upper Saddle River, New Jersey 07458

FT Press offers excellent discounts on this book when ordered in quantity for bulk purchases or special sales. For more information, please contact U.S. Corporate and Government Sales, 1-800-382-3419, corpsales@pearsontechgroup.com. For sales outside the U.S., please contact International Sales at international@pearsoned.com.

Printed in the United States of America

First Printing April 2008

ISBN-10: 0-13-235463-2
ISBN-13: 978-0-13-235463-9

Pearson Education LTD.
Pearson Education Australia PTY, Limited.
Pearson Education Singapore, Pte. Ltd.
Pearson Education North Asia, Ltd.
Pearson Education Canada, Ltd.
Pearson Educatión de Mexico, S.A. de C.V.
Pearson Education—Japan
Pearson Education Malaysia, Pte. Ltd.

Library of Congress Cataloging-in-Publication Data

Gunther, Robert E., 1960-

The truth about making smart decisions/ Robert E. Gunther.

    p. cm.

ISBN 0-13-235463-2 (pbk. : alk. paper) 1. Decision making. I. Title.

HD30.23.G86 2008

658.4'03--dc22

2007034060

Vice President, Publisher
Tim Moore

Associate Publisher and Director of Marketing
Amy Neidlinger

Acquisitions Editor
Jennifer Simon

Editorial Assistant
Pamela Boland

Development Editor
Russ Hall

Digital Marketing Manager
Julie Phifer

Marketing Coordinator
Megan Colvin

Cover and Interior Designs
Stuart Jackman,
Dorling Kindersley

Managing Editor
Gina Kanouse

Senior Project Editor
Lori Lyons

Copy Editor
Karen Gill

Design Manager
Sandra Schroeder

Senior Compositor
Gloria Schurick

Proofreader
San Dee Phillips

Manufacturing Buyer
Dan Uhrig

For my wife, Cynthia.
Marrying you was the best decision of my life.

Preface

Think quickly. Should you buy this book? You have to make a decision. Every minute of every day, you are making a series of small decisions that could change the course of your career and your life. Our lives are the sum of our decisions. Your success is largely a result of the quality of your decisions. Have you given any thought to how you make decisions?

This book won't keep you from making stupid decisions. Alas, it won't offer you a life without regret or buyer's remorse. It will help you step back from the heat of decision making and think about *how* you approach decision making. I've had the opportunity to work with some of the leading researchers in the field of decision making, including Paul Schoemaker, author of *Decision Traps* and *Winning Decisions*, Howard Kunreuther, co-director of the Wharton School's Risk and Decision Processes Center, and Jerry Wind and Colin Crook, authors of *The Power of Impossible Thinking*. I have learned a great deal from them about making decisions.

I wish I could say that all this good schooling has kept me from making absolutely disastrous decisions, but I'd be lying. I've walked away from a stable job to start a business (turned out to be a pretty good decision). I've moved 2,000 miles from Pennsylvania to Colorado with a St. Bernard and three kids and back again in one year (a disaster but a fascinating adventure as well). It is a decision I'd make again in a heartbeat because it was for the sake of family. So the little knowledge I have hasn't kept my tail out of the fire. But the way I think about and approach decisions has changed.

There is no simple formula for decisions, but we can become better at making them. No decision is perfect, but often doing nothing is worse. The time to act is now. On the following pages are a series of sharp insights that will give you new ways of thinking about your decisions. There are no shortcuts or machines to make decisions for you. You just need to dig in, open your eyes and get to work. I hope the following truths about decision making can help you in making your own tough decisions.

But some decisions are not all that tough. I mean, buy the book already.

—Robert Gunther

Introduction

In his '50s, after leaving the White House, President Theodore Roosevelt was faced with the opportunity to explore the Amazon in South America. The journey down the appropriately named River of Doubt (now Rio Roosevelt) was a prospect that was fraught with danger and almost killed his son Kermit. This was a time when the twenty-sixth U.S. president could have basked in the glory of his past achievements, writing his memoirs and putting his presidential library in order. A careful and calculating decision maker might have weighed the risks against the opportunity and wisely decided to stay at home. Roosevelt was not that kind of man. You can almost hear him responding enthusiastically with a single word: "Bully!" He said the trip made him feel like a boy again.[1]

There is an underlying assumption in much of the decision-making literature that making decisions should be based on a rational process. We know that it isn't, but these detours from rationality are usually seen as obstacles to effective decision making. And they certainly can be. Rational approaches also represent the part of decision making that is most easily trainable. We can recognize how problems such as overconfidence or *groupthink* cloud our judgment, as we will consider later in this book. It is important to recognize these challenges, particularly for large decisions that need to be carefully thought out. But it is also important to recognize that none of this would have led Roosevelt into the Amazon, for better or worse, or to the other wild successes of his hard-riding career.

This aspect of decision making is captured in the popular MasterCard commercials. While we can put price tags on some things, others defy this process. You might see Roosevelt tallying up the risks and costs of his trip on one side—the boat, the guides, the mosquito netting. On the other side would be the chance for a 50-something-year-old man to feel like a boy again: priceless.

This is what is so shocking about Malcolm Gladwell's observations in *Blink*.[2] He shows how a moment's intuition can sometimes be better than months of study and careful analysis. We can't assume that every decision can—or should—be made in this intuitive way. Shooting from the hip can sometimes get you killed. In *Th!nk*, a book-long response to Gladwell, author Michael LeGault blames fast and loose, nonlogical thinking for everything from declining student performance to failures of emergency response to the potential collapse of civilization.[3] There are hard problems that demand a more rational approach. Diagnosing and solving problems in a system or machine usually benefits from a rational approach. You may want your auto mechanic to have good intuition, but you also want him to be able to hook up the engine to a computer to find out what's wrong.

On the other hand, as we will consider in some of the Truths of this book, we tend to be somewhat risk averse as a species, and a systematic and logical approach may actually make us overcautious. By all means, look the decision squarely in the face. Consider it from every angle. But also focus on the intangibles that might be harder to place into a systematic equation of risks and returns. After you've done all this careful analysis, step back. Ask yourself: What would Teddy Roosevelt have done? If you hear the word "Bully!" going through your head, maybe the crazy decision is the right one. Don't underestimate the power of deciding boldly.

As Roosevelt said, "Far better it is to dare mighty things, to win glorious triumphs even though checkered by failure, than to rank with those poor spirits who neither enjoy nor suffer much because they live in the gray twilight that knows neither victory nor defeat."

TRUTH

1

Before a major decision,
get some Z's

This sounds like something your mother would tell you, but now Mom has a team of researchers at her side to back up what she says. Studies show that students who get enough sleep before a test can achieve higher grades—even if they don't study more. One of my study partners in college used to keep a jar of No-Doze on his desk and offer them around like candy during study sessions. Maybe he would have been better off just turning in early and arriving at the exam well rested.

Sleep deprivation, on the other hand, can lead to disastrous decisions. Three Mile Island happened on the night shift. Some of those who decided to launch the Challenger space shuttle had been awake for 72 hours. U.S. transportation studies find drowsiness a factor in nearly one-quarter of highway crashes and near accidents. Staying awake for more than 22 hours leads to the equivalent psychomotor performance of a 0.08 blood alcohol concentration. If you have a choice, wait until you have a good night's sleep. If you have a big decision, don't sit up all night worrying about it. Write it down and revisit it in the morning.

"Never make a serious decision when you are exhausted, tired, or sleep deprived," said David F. Dinges, Ph.D., chief of the Division of Sleep and Chronobiology and head of the sleep lab at the University of Pennsylvania. "That is a Russian Roulette game. We will all make mistakes by virtue of our biological limits when we are sleep deprived."

While ample rest is a simple idea, it's hard to do in our 24/7, venti-double-latte-driven world. From a practical standpoint, it's not always easy to get a good night's sleep. But if you don't sleep, don't decide. Pay attention to your level of fatigue and make your decision when you're well rested, if at all possible. Remember, huge disasters such as the Exxon Valdez oil spill and others were based on decisions made by managers who were very short on sleep.

Never make a serious decision when you are exhausted, tired, or sleep deprived.

The bottom line is to pay attention to your physical state when you're making a decision. Are you dog tired? Your physical condition will affect your decisions. If possible, make sure your eyes are wide open before you step onto the court.

TRUTH

2

Act from a state of clarity

There is a famous story about English inventor Elias Howe, who created the first practical sewing machine using a lock-stitch design. The design came when he was struggling with the question of how to design an efficient sewing machine with a standard sewing needle, which has the hole in the tail end.

During a dream one night, he was in a jungle surrounded by cannibals carrying spears. They ordered him to invent the sewing machine by morning, or he would be eaten. In the morning, the cannibals surrounded him, prepared to carry out their threat. As they were thrusting the spears at him, up and down, he noticed something strange. Every spear had a hole in the tip. He woke up and had the answer to his dilemma. He put the hole in the point of the needle and created a successful sewing machine. A problem that his conscious mind could not resolve was sewn up in his sleep.

The best ideas often come in the shower, while running, or even in dreams. Why? During those times we're able to relax and focus in ways that aren't possible with all the distractions of the modern office. Thomas Edison used to sit in a chair holding a weight in each hand. Just before he would doze off, he would drop the weights on the floor, and it would wake him. He could then benefit from the ideas formed in that twilight zone between sleeping and waking. This state of mental acuity is important to making good decisions. We are able to act from a state of clarity.

> A problem that his conscious mind could not resolve was sewn up in his sleep.

In her work with hundreds of executives, reinforced by research in neuroscience and sports physiology, Luda Kopeikina, CEO of Noventra Corporation and author of *The Right Decision Every Time*, identified acting from a state of clarity as a foundation for good decisions.[4] Just as athletes are able to achieve a state of focus and mental concentration to play at the top of their game, managers can cultivate clarity to improve decisions. This clarity comes from training the mind to be precise and accurate, as well as balancing body, mind, and emotions.

But our modern work environment seems designed to undermine clarity. Frequent interruptions, multitasking, stress, and fatigue work against clarity. Managers need to counter these forces to achieve a mental state that allows for reaching a clear decision. Sometimes if you can get your mind in the right place, the answer will follow.

Sometimes if you can get your mind in the right place, the answer will follow.

If you're facing a big decision, and particularly if you're stuck, check your state of mind. Are you acting from a position of clarity? Even if you're pressed for time, or someone is on the other end of the phone demanding a decision—yes or no—you can still find clarity. Just take a few deep breaths or ask a question to give yourself space to gain clarity before deciding. Don't use lack of clarity as an excuse for not making a decision, but try as much as possible to reach a state of clarity before you reach a decision.

If you hit a brick wall, put down the sledgehammer. It often won't yield to brute force. First find clarity. Then the wall will come down, and you can make your decision.

TRUTH

If you can't get distance,
get perspective

When writer Gay Talese faced a tight deadline for an article, he would sometimes hang up the typewritten copy of his story on the far side of his study and read it through a pair of binoculars. Through this lens, the copy looked printed. It literally allowed him to see it through a fresh set of eyes. It gave him a sense of detachment and "distance" when there was not time to put the manuscript away for a month.

It would be nice if we could put every decision away for a few days before making it. It would be nice to spend a few days meditating in the Nevada desert before making a choice. We might make much better decisions. But time is short for most decisions. The car salesman wants your answer before you walk out of the showroom. You need to decide on whether to take a job. You need to proceed with surgery right now. Deadlines have come and gone. You need to decide well, but decide quickly.

If you can't get the time and distance away from the decision, find ways to quickly get perspective, like Gay Talese did. This can be done by something as simple as talking to a colleague or friend to get a new view of the situation. Stand up and walk down the hallway. Changing your physical location can sometimes help. Make an excuse to get out of your office.

Take a walk. Do five or ten minutes of meditation. Visualize waking up in your world if you make the decision one way, and then visualize life with a different decision. Which picture is better? If you don't mind appearances, you might even take a page from Talese and post the decision on a far wall. Then look at it through binoculars.

> If you can't get the time and distance away from the decision, find ways to quickly get perspective.

Look for metaphors or analogies. How is this decision like other decisions in different industries and contexts? For example, is the decision to hire a new employee like choosing a partner in personal life? What can we learn from that personal decision that might be valuable in the professional one? Taking the decision out of your context into a new one can help to give you new perspectives on it.

You can't always climb to the top of Kilimanjaro to take a new look at the world. But you can move your mind to take a new look at your decision.

Visualize waking up in your world if you make the decision one way, and then visualize life with a different decision. Which picture is better?

TRUTH

4

Keep it real

Get real. If you want to consider a decision seriously, you need to move it from an abstract idea to a concrete reality. When motorists were asked about buying cleaner gasoline in the abstract, they were all for it, but when it came down to paying extra at the pump, that was another matter. Unless you are facing an immediate decision, most decisions are considered in the abstract. What will you do tomorrow or next year? Making decisions more concrete will change the way you approach them.

This can be seen in decisions about giving to charitable causes. People are much more likely to give to an identifiable victim than in response to compelling statistics. A study by researchers Deborah Small, George Lowenstein, and Paul Slovic found that when test subjects were given $5 and asked to make decisions about giving to a charitable victim, they were more likely to give if presented with the concrete image of a seven-year-old girl in Malawi than if presented a set of statistics about food shortages. This also explains why people gave $700,000 to young Jessica McClure after she fell down a well in Texas in 1987 or contributed almost $50,000 to save a single dog, Forgea, stranded on a ship in the Pacific Ocean. In fact, the researchers found that appealing to analysis by providing statistics actually decreased giving to an identifiable victim.

This concreteness is also key to the success of conjoint analysis, a marketing tool developed by Paul Green of the Wharton School that has been used to design new products from hotel chains to automobiles. Instead of asking consumers if they want certain features in the abstract—say a swimming pool or Internet connection at the hotel—*conjoint* forces subjects to make trade-offs between concrete options. They are given a choice between one hotel room with certain features at a certain price and another with a different set of features and pricing. The choices are then used to infer their preferences.

Because it is concrete, conjoint analysis can be more effective in understanding consumers than asking them straight out. For example, when a group of Stanford MBA students was asked what was most important to them in a job, they ranked salary far down on their list. Factors such as people and location were considered more important. Do you think it's surprising that MBA students, most with huge student loans to pay off, would not be more interested in salary? In fact, they are. But they don't want to appear to be. When the same students were surveyed using conjoint analysis, salary emerged as far and away the most important factor. The respondents didn't mean to lie, but they did. It was easy to rank order the goals in the abstract. It was much harder when dealing with concrete options.

You probably aren't going to commission a conjoint study every time you make a decision, but you can make sure you consider concrete options. First of all, when presenting yourself with a decision, try to put a face on the statistics. Tell a story and examine the impact of the decision on specific individuals. And put a specific price tag on the decision. What will it cost you? Are you willing to pay? Lots of decisions sound good in the abstract but turn out

When presenting yourself with a decision, try to put a face on the statistics.

to be disastrous. Make your decisions concrete before they actually become concrete. By "keeping it real," you will be more serious about the decision. You will be less likely to lie to yourself. You will think more carefully about the outcome and make better decisions.

TRUTH

5

Use a systematic process

Work the problem. A systematic process can help in making better decisions by helping to avoid or adjust for some of the biases in our thinking. It can ensure that you consider different options carefully and impartially and don't get too caught up in emotion or fall victim to other biases.

The classic rational process is to identify the problem (finding a bride, for example), identify the criteria for making a choice (intelligence, humor, romance), assign weights to the criteria (humor is more important than intelligence), find a process to generate alternatives (online dating service), evaluate each alternative (blind dates), and select the best choice (tie the knot).

> A systematic process can help in making better decisions by helping to avoid or adjust for some of the biases in our thinking.

In their book *Winning Decisions*, J. Edward Russo and Paul J. H. Schoemaker lay out a four-stage process for making decisions. The process begins with the divergent activities of framing and gathering intelligence. Framing sets the viewpoint and parameters of decision making. Gathering intelligence determines the facts and opinions that will inform the decision, as well as what is unknowable. This first part is about expanding options. The last two stages are the more convergent process of coming to conclusions and learning from experience to improve future decisions.

In their book *Smart Choices*, John S. Hammond, Ralph L. Keeney, and Howard Raiffa recommend using an approach they call PrOACT—problem, objectives, alternatives, consequences, trade-offs. This systematic approach can help in identifying what the decision is and specifying the objective, considering risk tolerance and looking at how what you decide on today influences what you may decide in the future.

Not all decisions are rational and systematic. When we worked through the selection of a marriage partner above, you may have been thinking that this rational approach was unrealistic. Did your own courtship proceed this way? I can tell you mine didn't. (It all started with a chance meeting by a young reporter after a frog jumping and turtle racing contest at a local 4-H fair, but that is a story for another day.) At the same time you are filling out your evaluation, your potential partners are filling out theirs. You need to select someone who also chooses you. (Otherwise, it's stalking.) It's not so much a decision process as a dance. Many decisions are like this—a somewhat orderly dance rather than a linear process.

We also have to beware of rationality. Often what appears to be a rational approach to decision making is actually something that's added after we've already made our decision. In this case, it's not rational, but rationalization. This is like when you decide you're going to hire a new employee or consultant based on past relationships and then lay out your arguments for doing so. You might shape the job description or request for proposals to give the desired candidate an edge. Then, surprise, this person is the best fit for the criteria! The rational part comes in after we actually make the decision.

Despite these caveats, there is great power in employing a systematic approach to decision making. This is particularly true when there is great complexity or there are serious consequences of the decision. When you can take the time, a rigorous process can help to shine light on complexity to keep from stumbling through the fog. A decision process is also important if you need to explain the decision to

> When you can take the time, a rigorous process can help to shine light on complexity to keep from stumbling through the fog.

others so that they are aligned in implementing it. If you are leading a platoon into battle or a company into the market, you owe it to the people behind you to have thought through the decision carefully. It also helps to slow down the process sufficiently to ensure that you look before you leap.

TRUTH

6

Know your
decision-making style

When I ask my wife how she makes decisions, she says she follows her heart. This is not just an excuse for bypassing formal, rational analysis that is such an essential part of classical decision making. It is also a sense that if you make a decision that you feel passionately about, you will put your heart and soul behind the decision. While I take a more rational approach, sometimes, I do appreciate where her heart has taken us.

Some people, like my wife, take an intuitive approach to decisions, while others would not think about making a decision without careful and formal analysis. These are very different styles of decision making. (In their book *The Dynamic Decision Maker: Five Decision Styles for Executive and Business Success*, Michael Driver, Kenneth Brousseau, and Philip Hunsaker consider a broader range of five different styles of decision making—decisive, flexible, hierarchic, integrative, and systemic.)

You need to understand your own preferred style of making decisions. Recognize that you're probably not a pure example of one approach or another. You might use different styles for different types of decisions. Some managers who pursue a rational approach at work might choose a more intuitive approach in making personal decisions. You also might choose a different approach for decisions under tight timeframes versus those with longer lead times.

> You need to understand your own preferred style of making decisions.

In addition to understanding your own style, you need to understand the styles of the people around you. If you're surrounded by logical decision makers, even if you arrive at your decision by intuition, you will want to present a logical argument for your plan. This might seem deceptive, but it could be the only way to get buy-in from people who expect decisions to be based on rational analysis. On the other hand, if you have to explain a rational decision to someone who is more intuitive or makes decisions based on feelings, you might need to find a way to appeal to the heart.

Recognizing your own style and those of others creates an opportunity to experiment with other ways of approaching decisions. Try a style that is not your natural one and see how it works out. It may be that you will want to incorporate it into your future decisions.

In addition to understanding your own style, you need to understand the styles of the people around you.

TRUTH

To make better decisions,
make more mistakes

This may seem counterintuitive because you might think you would get better at making decisions by avoiding mistakes. Not so.

In 1953, James Burke's career at Johnson & Johnson almost ended before it began. Shortly after arriving at the company, he was product director for several over-the-counter medicines for children. All of them were failures—multimillion dollar failures. He was called into the chairman's office, fully expecting to be fired. Instead, General Johnson told him that business is about making decisions. You don't make decisions without making mistakes. Just don't make the same mistake twice. And besides, the company had just invested millions of dollars in Burke's education. They were not about to let him go.

When have you learned the most in your career? Probably when you've made mistakes. One good mistake can teach us more than all the successful decisions combined. The trouble is that as we become older and more experienced, we take pride in the fact that we make fewer mistakes. We're good at what

> One good mistake can teach us more than all the successful decisions combined.

we do, and that means not screwing up, right? When we're toddlers, we trip and fall all the time. People think it's cute. When we grow up and stumble, it's not cute. We're punished, fired, and embarrassed. We become the butt of jokes, like President Gerald Ford ridiculed with stumbling pratfalls by comedian Chevy Chase. Mistakes hurt. The problem is that the fewer mistakes we make, the less we learn.

A less-talented leader than General Johnson might have fired Burke on the spot. By allowing Burke to make this huge mistake, Johnson advanced the career of an executive who would become one of J&J's greatest leaders and one of the most respected and courageous CEOs, named by *Fortune* as one of the "10 Greatest CEOs of All Time." General Johnson also helped create a culture that allowed for making mistakes. This was a lesson Burke never forgot. In 1982, he faced a crisis when seven people died in Chicago from Tylenol that had been laced with cyanide. It could have meant the end of the Tylenol brand, the country's best-selling over-the-counter pain reliever, or even the end of the company. Burke took a huge risk in recalling and repackaging millions of bottles of Tylenol. At the time, it was a controversial decision to put the company's ethics above profits. The out-of-pocket costs of the recall were immediate, and the returns were not at all certain. But Burke had spent his entire career making courageous decisions based on principle.

To make better decisions, you need to make mistakes. You also need to allow others to make mistakes. Do it in areas that are less visible and less risky. Don't bet your whole career or whole business (unless absolutely necessary). Don't drive your car over a cliff. Make mistakes, and visibly reward others who failed for the right reasons or succeeded by challenging a deeply held assumption that proved false. Ask yourself: How can you make more mistakes? Design experiments to test hypotheses (those you expect to work out) and then look for ways to take unexpected actions that you think may fail. You may be surprised by some unexpected successes that will change the way you look at your future decisions.

> To make better decisions, you need to make mistakes. You also need to allow others to make mistakes.

TRUTH

8

Be prepared to profit from your mistakes

It's not enough to make mistakes; you also have to be prepared to learn from them. There's an old story about a successful entrepreneur who spoke to a group of business school students. They asked him for the secret to how he earned his wealth. "Good decisions," he said. But the students pressed further: "How did you learn to make good decisions?" His answer, "Experience." But, asked one student, "Where did you get this experience?" His answer, "Bad decisions."

This is true only if you have a process to learn from your mistakes.

In his book, *The Go Point*, Michael Useem tells the story of Lenovo CEO Liu Chuanzhi, who founded one of the world's largest computer companies. Chuanzhi was not trained in business. He was working at the Chinese Academy of Sciences in 1984 when he formed the company that would become China's largest personal computer producer. How did Chuanzhi learn how to build a successful business with little or no business training? At the end of every week, Chuanzhi met with his top aides to review the major decisions they had made in the past week.

Systematically looking at their past decisions and learning from them was the equivalent of a business degree. They just kept getting better until they became one of the world's largest personal computer companies. In 2005, Lenovo acquired the personal computer business of IBM, the granddaddy of the personal computer. With constant practice and assessment of its decisions, Lenovo created a company that could take on the world. No matter where you start, you can keep improving your game by working on your faults and learning from your past mistakes and successes.

Take time on Friday afternoons or Monday mornings to review your decisions from the past week.

Take time on Friday afternoons or Monday mornings to review your decisions from the past week. You can do this individually or with other members of your team. What decisions did you make? How could you have made them better? How will this experience change the way you approach similar decisions in the future?

TRUTH

Learn from your close calls

Suppose that you consistently roll through stop signs when driving. One day, you are nearly broadsided by a Mack truck. But you narrowly escape with nothing more than a bruised ego from an obscene gesture from the other driver. What do you do? The typical reaction would be to wipe your brow and thank the road gods. Once your heart settles down, you would continue on without a second thought. Before you know it, you would be rolling through stop signs again—until one fateful day when the Mack truck actually makes contact. Then it would have your attention. Your driving would probably change (along with your insurance rates). This is just human nature. We tend to overlook the bad decisions that don't have disastrous outcomes but obsess upon those that do.

After the accident at the Union Carbide plant in Bhopal, India, the chemical industry reassessed its decisions about plant construction and management. After the meltdown at the Three Mile Island nuclear power plant in Pennsylvania, the nuclear industry went into its own meltdown. The Exxon-Valdez oil spill in Alaska forced a look at policies and the design of oil tankers. All these were catastrophic mistakes with serious consequences.[5]

We tend to overlook the bad decisions that don't have disastrous outcomes but obsess upon those that do.

There's another option. You could learn from your near misses. These are decisions that did not turn out too badly but could have been a lot worse. What can you learn from the near Bhopal's, the chemical leaks that were caught early and never made the headlines? What about the oil tankers that had an impaired captain at the wheel but didn't run aground? What about the nuclear accidents that didn't result in a TMI or Chernobyl? There are lessons in all these events, but we often don't receive these lessons because we escaped serious harm.

Companies in industries with risks of catastrophic events started looking at near misses, and this allowed them to learn from bad decisions before they became catastrophes.[6] These near misses never make the headlines. There is no meltdown or public relations disaster. But a lot of learning can take place, with only "homeopathic" doses of pain.

You can do the same. Look at the decisions you have made that resulted in near misses. Think about the lesson and change your behavior for the future. If you routinely arrive late for meetings and miss deadlines, and this behavior has led to cliffhangers but not outright disasters, what can you learn from this that will improve your decisions in the future? If you are the boss from hell and one of

> Look at the decisions you have made that resulted in near misses. Think about the lesson and change your behavior for the future.

your star employees leaves as a result—but didn't file a lawsuit— don't just count your lucky stars and hire your next casualty. Look for the lesson in what just happened.

What are the near misses in your own career or decision making? What can you learn from them? How can you use this learning to make better decisions in the future?

TRUTH

10

Learn from the decisions of others

While you should be sure to learn from your own mistakes, don't forget to learn from the mistakes of others, too. As Ben Franklin once said, "Experience keeps a dear school, but fools will learn in no other." Don't be a fool. Learn from the experience and wisdom of others.

Study the great mistakes of political, military, and business history. Why did Lee lose the battle of Gettysburg? Why was Custer's stand his last? How did Bill Gates and Warren Buffet build their fortunes? Make a study of crucial decisions and determine what contributed to their successes and failures.

Study the great mistakes of political, military, and business history.

Simulations and case studies can help you work through decisions and make mistakes without serious consequences. You need to take them seriously, maybe by putting a few real dollars into the game, but the lack of serious consequences allows you to experiment with new approaches. Firefighters engage in drills in houses filled with smoke so that they can move through their paces before it becomes a life-and-death matter. Pilots learn on flight simulators to address extreme situations that they hope they will never face in real life. Medical students test their skills on robotic patients.

While formal simulations can be expensive, cases and thought experiments are not. Read the newspaper and consider key decisions that are presented there. What would you do in this situation? Would you have made this acquisition? Would you have made the decision to go to war? What could you have done differently? What can you learn from these decisions to make better decisions of your own in the future?

You have time to make only so many mistakes in your own lifetime, as much as you might try. So learn from the mistakes of others. They can offer touchstones in making your own decisions better.

Simulations and case studies can help you work through decisions and make mistakes without serious consequences.

TRUTH

11

Don't judge your decisions based on their outcome

In his last movie, *Being There*, Peter Sellers plays Chance the Gardener, a dimwitted character who wanders out onto the streets of Washington, DC, and somehow manages to bumble his way to the heights of wealth and power. He doesn't even have the capacity to make good decisions. But everything he touches turns to gold. In the closing scene, he walks on water.

While few of us live such charmed lives, many times our bad decisions produce fantastic results. Sometimes the worst decisions turn out quite well. And sometimes good decisions lead to bad outcomes. You can't gauge the quality of the decision based on the way it turns out.

Just because the Challenger didn't explode after leaving the launch pad doesn't mean it was the right decision for the team to send it into orbit. They got lucky. There's an element of luck in the outcome of any decision. Accept it. Celebrate it. But don't confuse good outcomes with good decisions. Separate the outcome from the decision, or you'll never get better at making decisions.

> There's an element of luck in the outcome of any decision...But don't confuse good outcomes with good decisions.

That's easier said than done. It's human nature to be emotionally attached to the outcome of our decisions. If we get into Harvard or get the job of our dreams, it was the result of hard work and brains. If we don't, it was just bad luck. Success has many parents, but failure is an orphan.

Start by looking at your failures. The outcomes may have been poor, but if you were given the chance to do it over again, would you have made a different decision? Then look at your undeserved successes. If you succeeded, was it the result of the quality of your decision? What could you have done to improve the outcome?

Booking passage on the Titanic may not have been such a bad decision, given all the information known at the time; but it would appear to be a bad decision after the ship went down. Not bringing along enough lifeboats, however, does appear to be a mistake by the ship's owners and captain. It was one of many mistakes, fueled by overconfidence in this unsinkable ship, which contributed to the disaster.

To make better decisions, you have to step back from the outcome. Look at the quality of decision making and learn from it. You have to actively think about the process of decision making and the factors that lead to success and failure.

To make better decisions, you have to step back from the outcome. Look at the quality of decision making and learn from it.

TRUTH

Leave yourself room to get back from the pole

Do you have a margin for error? Mountain climbers know that the real trick is not getting to the summit but getting back down safely. When making a major decision, particularly a risky one, you need to have a plan to make your way back if it doesn't work out.

This was the difference between Ernest Shackleton and Robert Falcon Scott in their journeys to the South Pole. In 1909, Shackleton had crossed the Antarctic to within 97 miles of the pole. He had made it farthest south and would have been the first person to reach the pole if he had continued. He might have reached the pole, but he knew he couldn't bring his crew safely back. As he looked at his men, many suffering already from the ravages of cold and insufficient diet, he made the heartbreaking decision to turn around. He and all his men made it back safely.

Scott stood at the same point on January 9, 1912, three years to the day after Shackleton, but Scott decided to head on to the pole. With the failure of his horses and motorized tractors earlier in his trip, he and his men were forced to man-haul their sleds. They made it to the pole, but the entire party was lost on the way back.

This was also the mistake that Napoleon made in attacking Russia, stretching his troops and supply lines too thin against a fierce, entrenched enemy and brutal winter environment. Hitler didn't learn from this lesson and proceeded to repeat the mistake. Did they think carefully enough about what could have gone wrong and how they might recover?

How do you keep open a path of retreat? First, pay attention so that you can recognize when the decision you have made is not working out. What were the assumptions behind the decision? Have they been proven false by subsequent feedback? If you can identify the assumptions behind your decisions, you can recognize when those assumptions no longer hold.

One way to keep open a path of retreat is to build a margin for

> Pay attention so that you can recognize when the decision you have made is not working out.

error into your decision making. Roland Huntford, in his book *The Last Place on Earth*, detailing the race to the South Pole, notes the difference in margin for error of Robert Falcon Scott and Roald Amundsen. Amundsen prepared for the worst, carrying more than ten times more food and fuel per person than Scott and placing supplies far closer to the pole for his return. Scott expected the best and was disappointed when the unpredictable polar regions didn't cooperate. "In a journey of four months, Scott had not allowed for four days' bad weather," Huntford notes.

Amundsen made it back safely with food to spare. Scott and his men perished from starvation when they were pinned down by an extended storm.

Build a margin for error into your decision making.

Amundsen left a generous margin for error in other areas as well. As another example, consider how he marked his caches of food. Like other explorers, he ran supply missions out to bury food and other supplies in the snow and ice before making his primary push to the pole. Many explorers would mark these caches with a few flags in a sea of ice and snow. After reading about how others had missed or nearly missed these needles in haystacks, Amundsen came up with a system that gave his men more margin for error. He put flags on each cache and then ran a horizontal series of flags five miles on either side at half-mile intervals.

In considering any decision, ask yourself what could go wrong.

This gave his men a 10-mile target. Each flag was numbered so a traveler coming across a single flag would know exactly where to go to find the cache.

A margin of error allows you to recover more quickly or to survive if the decision does not work out as planned. In considering any decision, ask yourself what could go wrong. What would be your response? Do you have a plan B? A plan C? Have you thought through the various possible scenarios? How can you build a margin for error into your decision? Do you have a way back from the pole?

TRUTH

13

Understand common "decision traps"

You can't trust your own mind. We all make idiosyncratic mistakes in our individual decisions, but we share some common flaws that lead us into decision traps. In their classic book, *Decision Traps*, J. Edward Russo and Paul Schoemaker identified ten of the most dangerous decision traps in decision making:

- Acting too quickly or plunging in without giving sufficient attention to gathering information and deciding how to decide

- Solving the wrong problem due to frame blindness

- Having limited perspective and lack of "frame control"

- Displaying overconfidence in your judgment

- Being blindsided by conventional wisdom or other "shortsighted shortcuts"

- Shooting from the hip rather than using a systematic procedure

- Assuming that groups will make better decisions than individuals

- Failing to interpret evidence about past outcomes so you fool yourself about feedback

- Not keeping track of the results of your past decisions and learning from them

- Failing to audit your decision process and improve it

Understanding these and other traps (some of which are explored in more detail on the following pages) can help you recognize when you're about drop into one. This understanding can also help you think through strategies to prevent falling into these traps.

Remember how Odysseus, in the ancient story of his return from the Trojan War, was about to sail past the island of the sirens. Their voices were known for their unspeakable beauty, but they lured unsuspecting sailors to their deaths on the rocky shores of their island like moths to a flame. Since Odysseus was aware of this trap, as he approached

Think through strategies to prevent falling into these traps.

the land of the sirens, he plugged the ears of his men. He had them tie him to the mast, with orders not to release him no matter how much he pleaded. By knowing his own weaknesses, he could take steps to prevent falling into this trap.

Recognize the traps in your own thinking.

If you recognize the traps in your own thinking, you can effectively tie yourself to the mast to avoid falling onto these dark rocks.

TRUTH

14

Giving up something?
Get over it!

We hate to lose things. That's just human nature. Since the time we lost our first tooth, family pet, or game of baseball, we realized that losing hurts. We don't like to give up our money or our things. Is it any wonder companies end up overpaying for acquisitions? We hate to lose. And this aversion to loss affects our decisions in specific ways.

First, the loss aversion means that we value what we have to give up more than what we might gain—even if it is the same object or something as meaningless as a porcelain mug. In one study, half the subjects were given a mug and asked to sell it to the other half of the subjects. This was not a family heirloom, but just an ordinary mug they had acquired that day. But so strong is the desire not to lose things that the people who had the mugs actually valued them more highly than those who didn't. The have-nots only thought the mugs were worth an average of $2.50 to acquire. The haves wanted to receive $7 for each mug before they would let go of them. They scientifically verified the old saying that a bird in the hand is worth two in the bush. But in this case, the actual number was higher. A bird in the hand was worth almost *three* in the bush!

> We value what we have to give up more than what we might gain.

Studies by Nobel Prize winning economist Daniel Kahneman and colleagues found that the mean ratio of selling prices to buying prices was 2.29 across 16 experimental markets. This means that sellers expected to receive more than twice what the buyers thought the mugs were worth—merely because they had them in their hands!

This loss aversion also means that how you phrase a question affects the outcome. For example, people don't like to give up insurance coverage. In a Wharton study, half the subjects were asked if they wanted to *give up* some of their tort coverage in their insurance policies. The other half was asked if they wanted to *add* the coverage. The results should have been the same because they ended up with exactly the same coverage. But 77 percent of those who were asked to give up the rights held onto them compared to 44 percent of those who were asked to acquire them. Some of them probably didn't even know what "tort" was, but they had it and they wanted to keep it. This is human nature, but you need to understand it to make better decisions.[7]

Decisions often involve compromises. Ask yourself what you have to give up in making this decision. Then pose the decision in a different way. Put yourself in the buyer's shoes. Imagine that you don't have the thing you're being asked to give up. What would you pay to acquire it? This will help you filter out the blinders of loss aversion and make better decisions.

In his book *How to Stop Worrying and Start Living*, Dale Carnegie says one strategy for ending your worries is to stop worrying about a disaster and just imagine that the worst has already happened. Accept the worst and then try to improve on the situation. He tells the extraordinary story of a businessman with a severe ulcer that was considered incurable. His weight dropped from 175 to 90 pounds. He had to have his stomach pumped in the morning

> Just imagine that the worst has already happened.

and evening. And the doctors at the New York hospital still expected him to die. The man said that if he were going to die anyway, he had always wanted to travel around the world, so he was going on a cruise. The doctors warned him that he would die along the way, but with complete acceptance, he replied that he was bringing along his own casket. He had given the ship's captain orders to put him in the freezer if he died and take him home to his family plot. But he didn't need the casket. He pumped his own stomach every day at the start of the trip but soon began enjoying himself so much that he was eating everything—even the exotic dishes at their ports of call around the world. By the time he returned home, he was cured. He had accepted the worst and improved upon it.

Of course, knowing how averse we are to losing things won't make the process of giving them up any easier. So after letting go of something, get yourself some chocolate or a drink to ease the pain. Keep a stiff upper lip and let it go. Remember, it is only a stupid mug.

TRUTH

15

It's possible to miss an entire gorilla

How could you miss seeing a gorilla that is right in front of you? You could overlook a small spider, perhaps. A Chihuahua even. But a big, black, hairy gorilla would be impossible to miss, right?

Not so. In an experiment conducted by Daniel Simons and Christopher Chabris, the proverbial 800-pound gorilla was right there in the flesh, but subjects didn't see it.[8] Here's how the experiment went. The researchers showed participants a video of two teams playing basketball, one with white shirts and the other with black. The subjects were asked to count how many times the white-shirted players passed the ball. They dutifully complied, focusing on the white shirts. Bounce, bounce, bounce.

Most subjects came within one or two counts of the actual number of passes, but the majority missed something even more significant than getting the count right. A person in a gorilla costume walks right through the center of play. He even stops to beat his chest before moving on. There is a gorilla right in front of the subjects beating his chest. And they can't see it. What's wrong with this picture?

When we focus our attention on a specific area of the world or on a specific task, we can become blind to what's outside of it. This attentional blindness can cause us to miss significant issues that could affect our decisions. Where we look determines what facts we see. We're blind to the frames that we use. As every good magician knows, when we're focused intently on one thing, we may tune out other important signals.

Where we look determines what facts we see.

Most subjects who see the video again without counting don't believe it's the same film. They think there has been some sleight of hand. But it isn't sleight of hand. It's sleight of head.

We see what we look for. That's the bottom line. The subjects were so focused on the task at hand that they couldn't see the "gorillas in their midst" (as the study is called).

If you're immersed in a decision, particularly involving a task that requires a lot of attention, step back from it. Shift your focus and look at the bigger picture. Do you see something else? What gorillas are you missing?

52

TRUTH

16

You may see only what you're looking for

In his examination of how physicians think, physician and author Jerome Groopman notes that most physicians come up with two or three possible diagnoses within minutes of meeting a patient.[9] These decisions are influenced by the patients who came before, something known as an availability bias. We tend to try to fit the current situation to other examples readily available from our own experience.

For example, Groopman tells the story of a doctor on a Navajo reservation in Arizona who had seen dozens of patients over a three-week period suffering from viral pneumonia. So when a woman in her sixties complained that she was having trouble breathing, he determined that she had subclinical pneumonia. He made the diagnosis even though some of her symptoms and test results didn't fit this diagnosis (no signs of pneumonia on X-rays or elevated white blood counts). He ignored the facts.

> We tend to try to fit the current situation to other examples readily available from our own experience.

It was only after an internist looked at the results that he pointed out that the woman was actually suffering from aspirin toxicity. All the symptoms fit this diagnoses, and when the internist pointed that out, the doctor saw it instantly. But because of the other cases of pneumonia around him, he had missed it. This was a case where an experienced physician, relying on intuition or what he believed was a careful analysis of the situation, could be led astray by the cases that came first. He saw what he was prepared to see.

Some riddles are based on the same notion. (If red houses are made of red bricks, yellow houses are made of yellow bricks, and blue houses are made of blue bricks, what are greenhouses made of? While "green bricks" comes to mind, the answer, of course, is glass.) If you're launching a new business and three friends have just had to shut down their operations, you might overestimate the risks. On the other hand, if the three friends have achieved smashing successes, you might underestimate the risks. Neither view is the right one.

When you're making a decision, think about how your past decisions, your educational background, and your experience predispose you to look at the decision in a certain way. What could you see if you came to the decision fresh? What different decisions could this allow you to make?

TRUTH

17

You're not as clever as you think you are

In 1869, Major John Wesley Powell organized an expedition of ten men to explore the Green and the Colorado Rivers in the heart of the Grand Canyon. They traveled almost 1,000 miles by open boat through some of the most legendary rapids in the world. With the long journey and spoilage of their meager supplies due to moisture, their food was running out. There was no clear end in sight. After more than two months of battling the river, three men from the party took their leave of Powell at what became known as Separation Canyon. They told Powell, "We surely all will die if we continue on this journey." They were certain that the way forward meant death, so they decided to take their chances hiking out. But they were wrong. They were killed on their way out, probably by members of the Shivwits tribe.

Just three days after the separation, at the mouth of the Virgin River, Powell came across settlers fishing on the riverbanks. Powell and his remaining five crew members made it back safely. The three men who left the party based their decision on their confidence that they knew the way forward would be fatal. This was a miscalculation and a tragic example of overconfidence.

We all suffer from overconfidence. We're not as smart as we think we are. The brilliant Thomas Edison dismissed the phonograph as "not of any commercial value." Tell that to the music industry, which has topped $40 billion in the United States alone. While the technologies have changed, the industry is a direct outgrowth of Edison's "worthless" invention.

If you're human, you're probably overconfident, so take some actions to counter this tendency. Surround yourself with people who can challenge you and deflate your ego. (Spouses, children, and close friends often are quite adept at this.) Look at the facts. Powell, of course, tried to talk his men out of leaving the group. They might have listened to his arguments or considered that they would be better off remaining together than separating (or that Powell had managed to keep them alive through several months of the roughest whitewater). Get the facts instead of relying on guesswork. Sometimes a little bit of data can be

Surround yourself with people who can challenge you.

a sobering wakeup call. It can show how out of step with reality your own opinions may be. Be willing to be humble about your own level of knowledge.

Approach new challenges as a student and learner rather than an expert. (Remember that experts also tend to be overconfident.) It may be that you need to be willing to appear foolish to truly make wise decisions.

Approach new challenges as a student and learner rather than an expert.

TRUTH

18

Your view of the world depends on what planet you're from

My acupuncturist was trained in top Western medical schools before heading to Taiwan to study with Chinese masters of this ancient art of balancing energy through strategic placement of tiny needles. When I first went to see him, he remarked that he understands both Western and Eastern medicine but finds it almost impossible to explain one to the other. They represent different world views. Western medicine looks at attacking diseases through vaccines, pharmaceuticals, surgery, and other approaches. If there's a problem, you address the chemistry or remove the visible tumor. Acupuncture is based on balancing energy, or chi. The channels for this chi are not the same as nerve pathways. While we can't see this chi, it can be seen in the difference in a body that's alive versus one that's dead, even though the chemistry may be about the same.

This is a classic example of the power of frames. Frames limit what we can see. Sometimes we can't get there from here. In making a decision, our frames don't allow us to see a particular solution.

Frames limit what we can see.

When Intel's Andy Grove faced a problem with a flaw in the company's Pentium chip, he first viewed it from a technical standpoint. The 1994 "floating-point" flaw was initially dismissed as a minor problem that would affect only a few users. The company decided not to take action, other than to address the problem in future chips and not to disclose it. But what Grove and others failed to recognize was that Intel was shifting from a technology company to a consumer-facing company, as marked by its "Intel Inside" campaign. Through this new lens, the flaw was a serious consumer problem and a major public relations disaster. Customers demanded action. Intel finally changed its course, offering to replace every chip, resulting in a $500 million write-off on its 1994 revenue. The initial decision reflected a technical, internal view. The company's dismissal of the problem and lack of action made sense from this frame. The new decision could only be made after a shift in perspective to a more customer-facing view of the business.

Suppose you suffer from depression. If your question is, "What drug can I use to address it?" your answer will be a drug. But there are also approaches such as meditation and yoga that offer a very different view. Studies show that exercise and breathing can have a significant impact on health, particularly mental health. (If you doubt this, put down this book and go for a short walk. Then ask yourself how your perspective has changed as a result.) But while integrative approaches are becoming more common even in Western medicine, most diseases and treatments are seen through a narrow frame—a pill or procedure.

In addressing a decision, you need to recognize the lenses you use to view it. These lenses or frames limit how you pose the question and limit the questions you can see. How do you break out of these frames? The first approach is to seek out and immerse yourself in different views. It means achieving the "suspension of disbelief" that writers or playwrights seek when they invite you to visit their worlds. You can also explicitly recognize your frames. What are the limits of the education you received? What are the inherent limits of the way you were raised? What are other ways of looking at the same problem?

Seek out and immerse yourself in different views.

When I went to the acupuncturist for the first time, I was not at all convinced that it would be helpful, even though there was some research supporting it. But I considered the side effects as fairly minimal. I had several friends who had recommended this approach and this particular doctor. By the time I received the third recommendation, I decided to give it a try.

I still was reluctant to try this approach because I wanted to see clear empirical proof. This, of course, represented a limit in my own frame about medical decision making. We all make many decisions in our lives that are not based on clear empirical proof, and there's often a limit to the information we have access to. Lack of research and evidence, of course, can be a smoke screen for shoddy thinking and quack cures. But relying on rational thought alone as the only basis for decisions is a limited frame. As Santayana said, our goal is not to understand life but to live it. We live in the gray areas, so we need to act in a world that does not always offer sharp contrasts of

Relying on rational thought alone as the only basis for decisions is a limited frame.

black and white. Before making a decision, try entertaining different frames. If you see the world in black and white, shift your view from black to white; then try some shades of gray. This can help you to consider a broader set of solutions.[10]

TRUTH

19

Beware of seeing patterns that aren't there

Shortly after we were married, my wife and I moved into a small, second-floor apartment. The quiet, old gentleman who lived below us was mercifully hard of hearing, so he wasn't disturbed by our noisy cats thundering across the floor above his head. This neighbor passed away a few months after we moved in, and we were expecting the apartment to be leased again. One evening, I heard a loud radio blaring downstairs. The new people had arrived. The music continued through dinner, and I had a sinking feeling about the quality of our new neighbors.

But I was reluctant to make my first contact be a complaint about music. After all, we would have to live together, and they might not be so happy about having stampeding cats overhead. We might need some goodwill. So I waited through the evening. But the music didn't stop. I envisioned these hard-partying rockers downstairs—certainly rude and inconsiderate (and possibly armed and dangerous).

We crawled into bed, and the music was still playing. Finally at 1 a.m., I screwed up my courage and went down to confront the monsters. I knocked, but the door was open, so I pushed in. The apartment was completely empty except for some paint cans, drop cloths, and a boom box in the corner where the painters had left it. I shut off the radio and went to bed, feeling rather foolish.

I had based all my decisions throughout the night on my certainty that the music was coming from the new tenants. I had concocted this whole frightening portrait of these new neighbors based on the music coming from the floor below.

We as human beings are so good at making sense of the world that we often see patterns that aren't really there. We see "hot hands" in poker or "winning streaks" in basketball that are actually just statistical anomalies. We have a desire for coherent stories—the simpler the better—that explain reality. This is the miracle of seeing images in the inkblot test, clouds, or in the man in the moon. We are pattern-matching machines. Then we base our decisions on these stories we tell ourselves about reality.

We have to be careful to test our stories and our perceptions, as I finally did when I went down to confront the "neighbors." I could have done that earlier in the night. Instead of confronting them about the music, I could have just stopped by to welcome them to the neighborhood. We need to step back from our view of the world and test whether the patterns we see fit the picture.

We have to be careful to test our stories and our perceptions.

The incident with the new neighbor was a small mistake, but much bigger ones have been made on the same principle. (Think about the evidence that added up to a picture of "weapons of mass destruction" in Iraq that contributed to the U.S. decision to invade.) In any case, we often make decisions based on a certain view or story we've developed. First of all, we need to look creatively for other stories that might be supported by the same facts (a painter instead of an obnoxious neighbor). We also need to probe carefully for information that doesn't fit with the picture (paint fumes), and when we find these new pieces of the puzzle, we need to step back and see if our current story is the best one to explain what happened.

TRUTH

Different is not always better

You go to the same ocean resort for vacation every summer. You know your landlord and the local merchants. You know where to rent your bicycle and get your coffee in the morning. But this is the problem. These things are too familiar. So you decide to try something new and different.

Trying something different is harder than you think. First of all, there is a steep learning curve. You end up spending a lot of time finding out about the new location and finding a place to rent. Then you have to figure out where to buy your beach tags and purchase your suntan lotion. And it turns out that even after you sort things out, you don't have as good a time in the new location. (Of course, you also might have made a marvelous new discovery.) Was your decision driven by a need for variety? Do you think the grass is greener on the other side of the mountain?

Cherry is the most popular flavor of Lifesavers candies, but we often buy the five-flavor pack.[11] You may not care for orange, but you do like variety. Some of our decisions are driven by a need for variety, yet this doesn't always lead to better decisions. We see the negative side of this need for change in the management fads that sweep through organizations—TQM, business process reengineering, one-minute management, downsizing, rightsizing, and outsourcing. There is always at least a kernel of truth to these new ideas, and sometimes more than a kernel, but they often take on the wildfire passion of Pet Rocks and Beanie Babies.

If you're making a decision to change something that works, you should be particularly careful about your motivations. Recognize that you might be choosing something different merely because it's different. Is the new option that you're choosing really an improvement, or are you merely seeking variety? Is there another way to fulfill this need for change—such as taking up a new hobby rather than reorganizing the firm—that will lead to a better outcome?

Is the new option that you're choosing really an improvement, or are you merely seeking variety?

TRUTH

Boil knowledge down to its
essence—and then act on it

Few subjects are more complex than nutritional advice. Every week there is some new diet based on blood type, eliminating this food or that, or evoking scenes of bikini-clad sunbathers. And every week, there is some new study that shows that some food, such as butter, is bad for you. And then the next week, we read: Oh, wait, maybe it's not so bad after all.

In his wide-ranging discussion in *The New York Times Magazine*, Michael Pollan (author of *The Omnivore's Dilemma*) boils down his nutritional advice to a simple statement: "Eat food. Not too much. Mostly plants."[12] He goes on to recommend that we not eat anything that our great-great-grandmother wouldn't have eaten. This distills his complex topic of nutrition (a list of the antioxidants in thyme alone goes on for eight lines) and the often-heated debate over processed, vitamin-fortified "food."

What Pollan offers is a simple heuristic that distills three decades of research on food and nutrition into an actionable set of principles. It actually allows readers to make decisions about what to eat. Compare this to the never-ending and overwhelming stream of research and opinion in the popular media. Oats were added to almost everything, and now Omega-3 is the new savior of nutrition. The sheer quantity and diversity of information becomes overwhelming, so people throw up their hands and head for the McDonald's drive-thru.

> The sheer quantity and diversity of information becomes overwhelming.

In dealing with complex issues, a simple heuristic for decision making can keep you from being overwhelmed by the data. In venture capital and entrepreneurship, the heuristic might be "to fail fast and fail cheap." This conserves resources and speeds up learning. In the 1960s film *The Graduate*, one well-meaning adult boils down his advice for success to the young Benjamin Braddock (played by Dustin Hoffman) to one fateful word: "plastics." That is about as simple as it gets.

When you're facing a complex and confusing decision, see if you can come up with a simple principle (or heuristic) you can follow.

The surprising conclusion reached by Robert Meyer and Wesley Hutchinson of the Wharton School is that the simple heuristics used by managers to make decisions often lead to surprisingly good results.[13] Managers who are constrained by time and attention often don't go through a rational process of decision making. This is particularly true in multistage decisions that involve looking at the future. But managers can make the wrong decision at first and learn over time to arrive at more optimal decisions. They are, in the words of Meyer and Hutchinson, "bumbling geniuses."

When you're facing a complex and confusing decision, see if you can come up with a simple principle you can follow.

In using such shortcuts, we need to be sure we are in an environment that will give us the feedback needed to learn from our past decisions. If we are in a foggy or ambiguous environment, we may not be able to improve our shortcut or recognize when it is leading us astray.

The other trick to watch for with heuristics is that the world sometimes changes. New information arrives that might challenge this heuristic. If you come down with cancer or diabetes, you may need to change your decisions about diet and exercise. The simple rules can make it harder to see new information and act on it. In the workplace, the salaryman in Japan or the company man in the U.S. faced this situation when the standard rule for getting ahead—find a good company and move up the career track—was challenged by layoffs and reorganization. (By the way, they were, in fact, salary "men," which was one of the limits of the view.) The new compact has led to a "You, Inc." heuristic—where employees try to develop as much experience and skills as they can while moving across several organizations. So you need to be vigilant in determining whether your rules still fit as the world changes.

TRUTH

22

Decisions are not snapshots but movies

Mark Twain once said, "The art of prophecy is difficult, especially about the future."

There is never a crystal ball to figure out where each road will lead. A college dropout such as Bill Gates can go on to become one of the richest and most successful businessmen in the world. What parent wouldn't be concerned about a child dropping out of Harvard? How could Stephen King's mother know that the clippings she came across in his room about brutal killings were not the beginning of a career of crime but rather the genesis of great thrillers? The end is not always obvious from early decisions.

In considering decisions, we often look at snapshots rather than movies. We look at one decision but, in reality, each decision is part of a whole chain of decisions. Each decision we make today opens up other decisions tomorrow. The decisions snake out like a set of highways.

Sometimes decision makers capture these multistage decisions with formal decision trees, with weights on the different branches. For example, the high school student has to decide whether to finish school.

> Each decision we make today opens up other decisions tomorrow.

The graduate can then decide to go on to college or go directly to work or military service. The college graduate is then also faced with a fork in the road—pursue an advanced degree to join the workforce or even go traveling or to live on an ashram in India. In moments of decision, we often stand like Robert Frost considering "the road not taken," but do we carefully think through where each decision will lead?

We can think forward about our decision in three concrete ways. First, we can look at the way our decisions create "options" in the future. There is a whole field of management strategy focused on "real options," small investments today that create options for the future, similar to financial options. We can do this informally with all our decisions. For each decision, think about the options it creates for the future. How valuable are these options? When can you realize them? What do you need to do next? Think about how you can build decision points into the process so that you revisit the decision.

For example, a student might revisit career plans after every year of schooling. You might use an annual performance review at work to engage in your own review of your career decisions. (Unless you're hopelessly unromantic, however, do not use your wedding anniversary as an opportunity for a hard look at the relationship!)

Second, identify in advance when you need to pull the plug. There is no shame in making bad decisions. The problem is that we are likely to stick with a bad decision because of "sunk costs" and other factors. I once owned a 2000 Saab 9-5 that I bought when it was about a year old, so we didn't have a sense of its track record. (We later saw it turn up in a *Consumer Reports* list of worst used cars to buy.) Everything went wrong with this car, from broken seat belts and instrument panels to a door handle that broke off. The "performance" tires failed every time they hit a pothole. Finally, we had to replace a $2,000 computer chip for the braking system. We faced more failures, but we had invested so much that we felt we couldn't walk away. In the end, one bleak November evening, the catalytic converter caught fire, and we called the fire department. We didn't give up on the car. It had finally given up on us—in a blaze of glory. We should have walked away long before, but we couldn't bear to part with our past investments until the fire trucks arrived. This is the sunk cost fallacy, and it is just one of the reasons that it's hard for us to walk away from bad decisions or kill the ones that aren't working out. If we had said to ourselves, "If we face a repair above $1,000, that's it," we might have been able to walk away. Your past decisions weigh upon your future decisions.

> Identify in advance when you need to pull the plug.

Finally, for any decision, think through the next steps. What opportunities will this decision open in the future? What are the next decisions you'll be faced with? If you play chess, think about the series of decisions and how they might play out, given the expected moves on the board in reaction to your first move. If you're a movie buff, figure out what story you're in and where it might lead (of course, remembering that life rarely turns out the way it does in the movies). Where is the story headed and how could it turn out differently?

TRUTH

No decision is an island

Your decisions affect the world around you, which, in turn, affects the value of your decisions. Confused? Consider this question: Is it a good idea to wear a bicycle helmet? This seems like one of the simplest decisions. A no-brainer (literally). Helmets protect your skull and make it more likely that you will survive a crash. But among cyclists who ride on city streets, there is also a belief that wearing a helmet makes you more likely to be hit by a car.

Are these cyclists crazy? It turns out that maybe they aren't. Ian Walker, a psychologist at the University of Bath, decided to put these competing theories to the test.[14] He rigged up his bike with sensors and took to the roads. His experiment—comparing rides with a helmet to those without—found that motorists gave him a wider berth when he had no helmet. They passed more than 3 inches closer when his head was protected. So putting on safety gear actually increased his risk of being hit. Walker theorized that drivers viewed cyclists with helmets as more experienced and so required less caution. He reached the controversial conclusion that it might actually be safer to leave his helmet behind.

Our actions change the world around us. Werner Heisenberg found that it was impossible to know the position and momentum of an electron because the very act of measuring changes it. This "observer effect" contributed to quantum physics, which is based on probabilities rather than the more straightforward Newtonian universe.

Our actions and decisions change the world around us. We need to be aware of how these changes

Our actions change the world around us.

affect the environment and how the environment affects the outcome of the decision. It may have been a great decision for Monsanto to create genetically modified seeds and foods, but the benefits were substantially diminished when activists labeled such products "Frankenfoods" and actively opposed them. No decision is made in a vacuum, and there are ripple effects that can change the outcome. Sometimes the environment contains tractor-trailer drivers who are making their own decisions about how to react to a cyclist on the road ahead. This means that straightforward decisions such as wearing a bicycle helmet may not be so simple after all.

In making a decision, consider others who will be affected by the decision. What will be their reaction? How could this reaction change the outcome of the decision? Can you shape or change those reactions? (In his bicycle helmet study, Walker suggested mounting a government advertising campaign to urge motorists to give helmeted cyclists just as much space on the road.) Is your original decision still a good decision given these expected reactions?

No decision is made in a vacuum, and there are ripple effects that can change the outcome.

TRUTH

Build the city around your decision

James Jerome Hill was born just three decades after Lewis and Clark first blazed trails across the United State to the Pacific. After success in steamboats and other businesses in St. Paul, Minnesota, Hill decided to build a railroad across the prairies of the West. The Canadian Pacific and Northern Pacific lines had already reached the West coast, built with government support, so many thought it was foolish for Hill to attempt to revive the St. Paul and Pacific railway backed by private investors. But Hill ultimately created a network of 6,000 miles of tracks crossing Minnesota, Dakota, and Montana to the Pacific Ocean. Completed in 1893, the Great Northern Railway (which later became part of Burlington Northern) became the first transcontinental railroad constructed without government aid.

But to make the railroad a success, Hill focused on building towns along the route. The trains had to go somewhere, so he built the destinations. He offered breeding stock to farmers and sent out demonstration trains to show settlers better farming methods. He built grain silos. Soon, his rail lines were lined with farms, producing grain and livestock that Hill's trains took to market. When he reached the Pacific, Hill even looked beyond the borders of the United States, establishing a steamship line to Japan. He was soon doing $50 million per year in business with Asia. By consistently thinking beyond the decision at hand, Hill made his initial decision to build the railroad more successful.

Steve Jobs's genius in creating the iPod was not just in building an impeccably designed digital music player. He built an entire ecosystem around it. He looked beyond equipment (which was Apple's primary focus at the time) to manage content, create software that worked on the iPod and the computer (not just Macs, either), and line up a music library of songs from different labels that could easily be downloaded for just 99 cents. In designing this universe, Jobs did what the music companies were unable to do. It's unlikely that Apple's digital music player would have been such a success on its own, no matter how cool it looked. It was this entire system that made it a resounding success.

In making a decision, consider the factors that are needed to support the success of the decision. Are these factors under your control? Can you create a context for your decision that will ensure its success, as Hill did in building his railroad or Jobs did in creating the iPod?

TRUTH

25

Listen for the dog that doesn't bark

I recently had the opportunity to kayak down the Grand Canyon. There are plenty of real problems to worry about in that area. There are scorpions and 14 different kinds of rattlesnakes in the underbrush; a bite from any one of which might lead to a long and expensive helicopter ride out to a hospital. There are cliffs and rocks with the potential for broken limbs. And that's in addition to some of the biggest water in the West, which offers at least a small threat of drowning. In other words, my Grand Canyon kayaking trip offered plenty of ways to be injured or killed.

What actually almost killed me had nothing to do with the risks that I had identified before I left. It was not rattlesnakes or Class 10 rapids. (They use a different scale on the Colorado River.) It was a simple toe infection that came from wearing water shoes for 17 days. When I returned, I had such a severe infection that one toe swelled to three times its normal size. My doctor said I was at risk for a blood infection and probably should have been hospitalized. A series of horse needles full of antibiotics in my rear finally brought it under control. The dangers I had factored into my decision and that I had planned for were not the ones that I should have worried about most.

In Sir Arthur Conan Doyle's famous short story *Silver Blaze*, about the theft of a racehorse by the same name and the murder of its trainer, Sherlock Holmes points out to a Scotland Yard detective "the curious incident of the dog in the night-time." The detective replies, "The dog did nothing in the night-time." And Holmes replies, "That was the curious incident." The dog didn't bark because the beast knew the thief and murderer, which narrowed the list of suspects.

While Holmes is a fictional character, this type of information has serious implications in the real world. We are usually looking for the obvious signs—the smoking gun, the barking dog, the rushing rapids. We don't often ask ourselves, "What information is missing?" Sometimes, as with the barking dog, the missing information is just not there. Other times, there are people around us who make deliberate attempts to obscure it.

What information is missing?

For example, how many people were killed in the war in Iraq in its first four years? If you said more than 3,000, you're only looking at part of the data. That was the number of U.S. military casualties by late 2006. The Iraqi civilians and security forces killed in the war topped 26,000 in October 2005, according to the official U.S. government count. It could actually have been as high as 70,000 or even higher by mid-2007.[15] The data we look at are usually just U.S. casualties, but the broader data give a different picture of the war's impact. It could lead to different decisions if more attention were given to total casualties. This is the dog that didn't bark.

If I had been aware of the risk of toe infections on the Grand Canyon—so common it is called "*toelio*" by the river guides—I could have taken precautions to keep my feet dry. I could have treated myself in advance with antifungal creams, as I later found out that the more experienced among our crew had done. In other words, if I had "heard" the dog that didn't bark, I could have factored it into my decision or taken steps to keep it at bay.

When presented with a problem, we often accept the data as given. We collect it, or it is handed to us, and we then try to make the best sense of it. But to make better decisions, we need to begin asking, "What is missing? What can the missing data tell us? What one piece of information could change the way we look at this problem? Where can we get our hands on this information?" It may be that if we ignore the dog that doesn't bark, it could come back to bite us in the end.

> What one piece of information could change the way we look at this problem?

TRUTH

26

Sorry, Joe Friday. The facts
are never "just the facts."

"Just the facts, ma'am." The signature line of Dragnet's hardened detective Sgt. Joe Friday seems straightforward. With all due respect to Friday, nothing could be further from the truth. Data can be twisted and turned and reshuffled. As the old saying goes, if you torture the data long enough, you can get it to confess to anything!

Doctors were performing routine cancer screenings and expensive coronary bypass surgery until they took another look at the statistics. Dr. David Eddy estimated that as few as 15 percent of all medical protocols are actually based on sound data. These are doctors; professionals trained to make rigorous decisions. Do the rest of us have the faintest hope of success?[16]

Look at the quality of your data. If you put garbage in, guess what you'll get out? If you don't have good information, you can't make good decisions, but often we make assumptions about the quality of our information that aren't justified. People actually do rely on the Internet for medical information when much of it is not worth the pixels it is glowing on.

Statistics and other data can be a valuable resource in making a decision. But always consider the source. Is there an ulterior motive in offering a rosy picture or a dark picture? Where can you go for unbiased information? Does it exist? Even data sources that are not shaped by some nefarious motive can be limited in some natural way that obscures the true picture. Consider the biases that are inherent in your sources of information.

If you don't have good information, you can't make good decisions.

Then look elsewhere to get a fuller view. Remember that any gumshoe would tell you that you need to pound the pavement for information before you can track down a suspect.

TRUTH

Recognize the power of
intuition

We're all warned about not jumping to conclusions or judging a book by its cover. In fact, we usually buy a book based on the cover or make even more important decisions such as hiring a new employee based on initial, gut reactions. Often the results are not half bad, and sometimes they are better than careful, rational analysis. For example, in his book *Blink*, Malcolm Gladwell describes how the J. Paul Getty Museum spent 14 months carefully analyzing the authenticity of a Greek statue. A geologist analyzed a core sample from the statue and concluded that the stone was ancient, rather than a modern forgery. But later, a series of experts had immediate and visceral reactions to the statue. They were sure that it was a fake but couldn't explain why.

Starbucks founder Howard Schultz pursued his idea against all the best advice of his partners and those around him. With grounding in a certain discipline, we have the power to use our intuition to access our knowledge quickly. Gary Klein discusses how firefighters can make life-and-death decisions under time pressures. An experienced fire chief might sense a problem and pull his men out just before a building collapses.

In some cases, intuition is built upon deep experience. It is not a casual process or a hunch about an area of limited expertise. Where the trouble can come in with intuition is when we apply it in areas where we don't have this deep knowledge. We're notoriously good at fooling ourselves into thinking we know more than we do. Remember our tendency to be overconfident. This means that we'll follow our hunches right off the edge into oblivion. In trusting our gut, we need to be careful at the same time about falling into traps in our thinking.

In some cases, intuition is built upon deep experience.

Another concern with intuition is that the world may change. David Ogilvy may have wonderful intuition about print or television advertising, but will these instincts hold in an online world? Don't be like my St. Bernard who still walks around in circles three times before going to sleep—presumably some ancient ritual to trample the grass to prepare for rest. He doesn't live on the plains but has a dog bed already prepared. However, we often hold to old intuition that is just as out of step with our current environment. We need to be careful of intuition when the game has changed.

But intuition, used well, can be a fast and powerful way to make decisions. Think about some of the most important decisions of your life, and you may find that they were based more on gut feeling than rational analysis. In making a decision, pay attention to what your intuition is telling you. What do you feel about this decision? What is your gut telling you to do? How is this different from the results of careful analysis? Can your intuition indicate something that you're missing?

TRUTH

28

The wrong decision is better than none at all

A Swiss army unit was hopelessly lost during survival maneuvers in the Alps. It was cold. The team had limited food. Then one of the soldiers found a map in his backpack. They followed the map and made it back to base camp. They were saved!

When their commander examined the map, he was shocked to find that they were following the wrong map. It wasn't a map of the Alps at all. It was a map of the Pyrenees. They had found their way back by following the wrong map. If they hadn't found the map, they might have spent hours or days waiting for help to arrive. Instead, they walked out. It's often better to move forward based on the wrong map than to sit still and starve. When all else fails, do something!

In kayaking, it's often a good idea to take your time picking your way through a rapid, stopping in eddies to inspect the next drop or scouting

When all else fails, do something!

from the shore. But when you're committed to big water, the best approach is usually to paddle like you mean it. Keeping your paddle in the water and moving decisively forward adds to the stability of the boat and improves your ability to maneuver.

This approach defies every instinct we have, of course. I remember that one of the spots I swam while kayaking in the Grand Canyon was a giant wave/hole at the bottom of a rapid called Hermit. The river guides had warned us that a 30-foot motor launch had been capsized by this monster, which had opened up when some rocks shifted the year before. Naturally, I paddled right into it. And my reaction was the typical deer-in-headlights response to staring into the mouth of such a beast. The next thing I knew, I was so deep in the water that there was no way out. But if I had resisted this state of shock and just paddled aggressively, I might have been able to punch right through it as others did.

In making decisions, we need to be cautious about falling prey to such paralysis. If you're facing a terrifying decision with serious implications, it's not the time to be faint of heart. Paddle boldy into it. If it's certain death to stay in your camp, then follow the map—even if it's the wrong map. You can correct your course on-the-fly. If you're perched on the precipice of a massive wave where there's no turning back, paddle boldly forward. Sometimes that act of bold commitment is what will lead you through the uncertainty of a difficult decision.

So if you're faced with a decision that is overwhelming in a way that leads to paralysis, if it's clear that the time for thinking is over and the time for acting has arrived, move forward with boldness. You may be following the wrong map but still arrive safely home.

> Sometimes that act of bold commitment is what will lead you through the uncertainty of a difficult decision.

TRUTH

Get 80 percent (or less) of
what you need, and then
act on it

You will never have all the information you need to make a decision. But if you wait for perfect information, the world will likely have changed. This is certainly true in heat-of-the-moment battlefield decisions. But even in more deliberate decisions, the gathering of data can become an excuse for not taking the risk of acting.

At a lecture I once attended, *Time* magazine White House correspondent Hugh Sidey compared the leadership styles of Presidents Jimmy Carter and Ronald Reagan. Carter, a nuclear engineer, was analytical. He gathered all the facts and carefully looked at every angle before making a decision. It often slowed his response. And he still ended up with a rescue team stranded in the desert on its way to free U.S. hostages in Iran.

In contrast, Sidey described the concern of staff as Reagan prepared for the historic disarmament talks with Mikhail Gorbachev. Stacks of background briefings sat virtually unopened on his desk. He would walk by and pat the stack of papers as he passed. And yet, Reagan walked into the meetings with his warm engagement and was able to hammer out agreements that led to the diffusing of the Cold War. When he returned, his staff was anxious to hear how he held his own in those private meetings. He replied that Gorbachev didn't know that much either.

It can be dangerous to shoot from the hip, but there are also dangers to analysis. In making decisions, you need to know how much information you really need and how long you can wait until you have to act. The goal is not to be perfect but to know enough and then move forward. Sometimes taking a decisive step forward can be more important than developing a Ph.D. thesis in getting the job done.

> You need to know how much information you really need and how long you can wait until you have to act.

Satisficing is what Nobel Laureate Herbert Simon called it. In contrast to optimizing, satisficing is figuring out the minimum requirements needed to be successful and then looking for the first alternative that meets those minimum requirements. This is particularly important in situations where the choices are complex or are presented one at a time.

Remember, if two tons of data fall on your head, it could lead to paralysis. Tools and data are good, but recognize that all the tools and data in the world can't make the decision for you. Managers still have to make the decisions at the end of

Don't ignore research, but don't be a slave to it either.

the day. And the tools can lead to "paralysis by analysis." Sometimes the best decisions run counter to the best research. Market research didn't see much of a market for the Walkman, but Sony's Akio Morita defied the research and launched a product that transformed portable entertainment and defined his company. Don't ignore research, but don't be a slave to it either.

TRUTH

30

Every decision carries risk.
Get used to it.

When I was in college, my roommate and I had often discussed the idea of buying a motorcycle. I happened to be the first one to land a cycle, a beat-up Honda with bald tires. Naturally, my first trip was three hours up the Garden State Parkway and New Jersey Turnpike to visit him. I lived in southern New Jersey, and he lived in Teaneck, just across from New York City. There seemed to be an unexpectedly large quantity of 18-wheelers on the turnpike, generating buffeting winds. But I made it safely, my roommate was suitably impressed, and we had a wonderful visit. I knew the bald tires wouldn't be much of a problem—as long as it didn't rain.

As I roared south, I ran into a near-hurricane. Thunder crashed. Lightning lit the sky. As the rain cascaded down, cars pulled over onto the side of the road. I thought about doing the same, but I didn't see the wisdom of it. In the middle of the Pine Barrens, I could only get more soaked, so I continued slowly, miserably onward. I made it safely home, perhaps a bit humbled by the experience but also exultant as I listened to the rain hissing on the hot engine when I headed inside the house.

In retrospect, I knew I'd made some risky decisions. My first risky decision was to buy the motorcycle. The second risk was to take my first trip to a crowded metropolitan area, and the third was to head back in the rain with bald tires. Very often with a motorcycle, you get only one serious accident. (I later spoke to a friend who had run into a deer. The deer walked away, but my friend spent months recovering.) However, I was comfortable with the risk involved and felt that the thrill of the wind racing past me was more than worth it.

Every decision carries risks, so you need to understand your attitude toward risk. If you have a low tolerance for risk, you might want to consider alternatives that are more solid and predictable in making your decisions. But you also should ask yourself whether you're too conservative. Is the sure thing really a sure thing? Are

If you have a low tolerance for risk, you might want to consider alternatives that are more solid and predictable in making your decisions.

the risks you perceive really so high? A more risk-averse friend once had the opportunity to buy a California condo years ago for about $300,000. Believing the real estate market was going to go south, he decided not to. The value of the property went up above $1 million.

Look carefully at the downside and consider whether you can actually live with it.

He may have been a little too risk averse (although if the market had gone bad, he would have been smiling all the way to bank).

If you have a high tolerance for risk, on the other hand, you will probably consider riskier alternatives in making decisions. In plotting your career, you might consider leaving the corporate path and setting up an entrepreneurial venture. You might opt for the long-shot investment or the bigger house, despite the chance of failure. If you're more comfortable with risks, you should be careful to ask yourself if you're taking unwarranted risks. Look carefully at the downside and consider whether you can actually live with it. Don't assume that all will turn out for the best. Talk to pessimists and consult with people who are risk averse. Speak to some people who have crashed their motorcycles. My father-in-law, who was a volunteer fireman, was a much more conservative driver because of responding to thousands of rescue calls. He knew what could go wrong. This doesn't mean you won't pursue a risky course, but you'll do so with your eyes open.

Finally, remember that risk is a part of life. It's tempting to think that you can analyze away or plan away all the risk in decisions. That's a trap. There's no way to take the risk out of decisions. Otherwise, there would be nothing to decide. You don't have to drive a motorcycle, but you still take risks even when you get behind the wheel of a Volvo loaded with airbags. Understand your attitude toward risk and factor this into your decision making.

TRUTH

31

Not making a decision
is a decision

The late Peter Drucker once wrote, "One has to make a decision when a condition is likely to degenerate if nothing is done....The effective decision-maker compares effort and risk of action to risk of inaction."[17]

Drucker recognized that there are risks to standing still. If you're unable to make the decision to accept a new job, you have rejected it by default. If you're unable to make an offer on a house, someone else may snatch it from under you.

Make your decisions explicit. Instead of allowing decisions to happen, be sure you take an active role in making them. This way you don't give up your power to make decisions. It's also healthier to be in control of your own destiny. When I say "healthier," I don't mean figuratively. Professor Marty Seligman, author of *Learned Optimism*, conducted early studies with animals that experienced what he called *learned helplessness*. In this case, they were given shocks that they were unable to control. One of his graduate students, Madelon Visintainer, did a similar experiment with rats who were injected with cancer cells that would be expected to give half of them cancer under normal conditions. She placed one-third of the rats in a control group and another third in a helpless situation where they were shocked without any way of preventing it. They learned helplessness. The last group of rats was given shocks but could stop the shocks by pressing a bar. They were able to achieve mastery over the situation. In the control group, half the rats developed cancer, as expected. For the rats that had learned mastery (with the bar), about 30 percent got cancer. But for the rats that had learned helplessness, more than 70 percent developed cancer. While such a study can't be explicitly replicated in humans, Seligman found similar effects in subsequent human research. It argues for taking an active role in your decision making.

> Instead of allowing decisions to happen, be sure you take an active role in making them.

Active decisions give you a feeling of mastery over the situation at hand. This will lead to better decisions—and perhaps even better health. Challenge yourself to make clear decisions. Don't procrastinate, sit on the fence, weasel, or waffle. If you make a mistake, pick yourself up and continue onward.

Standing still can be just as risky as moving in the wrong direction. As Will Rogers once said, "Even if you are on the right track, you'll get run over if you just sit there."

Standing still can be just as risky as moving in the wrong direction.

TRUTH

Two heads can be worse than one

How did the U.S. get into the war in Iraq? The best minds of the nation were focused on this topic for weeks. Top leaders made pitches. Journalists wrote stories. Hundreds of members of the U.S. Senate and Congress should have served as a check, but they waved it on. Since the problem was framed as a battle between freedom and terrorism, who wanted to be on the wrong side? Our allies around the world, with a few notable exceptions, either got in line with the "coalition of the willing" or diplomatically kept quiet. Those countries who didn't participate, such as France, were left holding their "freedom fries."

The decision of the United States to invade Iraq was originally justified based on the belief that there were "weapons of mass destruction" in Iraq. This conclusion was reached based on intelligence that had come in from different sources, but the evidence soon evaporated. The weapons were never found.

Even the news media, the fourth estate that should be a watchdog on policymakers, failed to ask the probing questions (as recognized when *The New York Times* actually made a public apology). This was a case where some careful probing might have revealed a very different picture. The kindest view was that this was a reflection of the difficulty of making sense from the foggy information that emerges from intelligence sources. The less favorable view was that the story was designed as a rationale for a foregone conclusion that the invasion was the right thing to do.

Weak information was strengthened. Weak arguments were glossed over. And we woke up several years later with a collective hangover and a serious problem next to us in the bed—and with no easy way out. This is groupthink at its worst.[18] Many people looked at the same problem, and they still made a decision that increasingly looks like a disastrous one. The Challenger space shuttle disaster is attributed to a similar desire to proceed that ran roughshod over the voices or potential voices of dissent. The desire for harmony and unanimity can overcome the careful thinking and conflict that could raise important questions and challenge the decision.

When making group decisions, examine the interactions of the group. Do they allow different voices to be heard independently? Do they allow the best ideas to percolate to the surface, or does one powerful voice dominate? If you have a leader in the room who is in a position of extreme power and influence, consider ways to get the leader out of the discussion. This could be by removing the leader

When making group decisions, examine the interactions of the group. Do they allow different voices to be heard independently?

from the room or by making a conscious effort not to dominate the discussion. You cannot underestimate the power of the leader. I remember a CEO who once reported that after he switched to wearing suspenders, he noticed that many other executives followed suit. If you're in a situation where everyone agrees on a decision, especially after little discussion or debate, you should get in the habit of asking, "What's wrong?" What questions are unasked, and how do you bring the revolutionaries into the room who will have the courage to ask them?

TRUTH

33

Use constructive conflict

There have been few more high-pressure decisions than those made in the U.S. White House in October 1962 during the Cuban Missile Crisis. With surface-to-surface missiles in Cuba pointed right at the U.S. backyard, the intense pressure was the only certainty. As Robert Kennedy commented in his memoir of the crisis, *Thirteen Days*:

"Each one of us was being asked to make a recommendation which would affect the future of all mankind, a recommendation which, if wrong and if accepted, could mean the destruction of the human race. That kind of pressure does strange things to a human being, even to brilliant, self-confident, mature, experienced men. For some it brings out characteristics and strengths that perhaps they never knew they had, and for others the pressure is too overwhelming."[19]

Sometimes groups can be smarter than individuals, particularly if structures are in place that allow all voices to be heard and their intelligence cleverly pooled. New Yorker writer James Surowiecki points out in his book *The Wisdom of Crowds* that a group can sometimes be smarter than its individual members.[20] This wisdom is seen in the success of Google's search engine, based on the searches of other users. As another example, while experts were correct only 65 percent of the time in answering questions from the game show *Who Wants to Be a Millionaire?*, the "less expert" TV studio audience guessed right 91 percent of the time. Although groups are susceptible to groupthink and other limitations that make them less smart than individuals, Surowiecki points out that "under the right circumstances, groups are remarkably intelligent, and are often smarter than the smartest people in them."[21]

> Sometimes groups can be smarter than individuals, particularly if structures are in place that allow all voices to be heard and their intelligence cleverly pooled.

Early in the crisis, President John F. Kennedy assembled his top advisors and asked them to work in small groups to develop independent recommendations, including talking points for a speech to the nation explaining the move and possible contingencies. The resulting plans ranged from a direct military attack on Cuba to a naval blockade of Soviet ships headed to the island. Despite differences in rank, the participants in the discussion all "spoke as equals." The president ultimately made the choice from the options, choosing a naval blockade of Soviet ships headed to Cuba as a first course of action. This still left open the option (and threat) of subsequent military action if the blockade was unsuccessful. This was a decision—and a series of subsequent decisions that followed—where the fate of the world was in the balance. The decision had to be right.

John F. Kennedy had learned from the disastrous decision he made earlier to launch the Bay of Pigs invasion of Cuba in 1961. This was a decision in which groupthink ruled the day. The plan was to train Cuban exiles to launch an attack on Fidel Castro's communist regime in Cuba. The decision was made by a group of top advisors to the president who came from very coherent backgrounds (similar universities) and who were reluctant to challenge him. None of the advisors felt comfortable in talking about the flaws in the plan, so it proceeded.

Few decisions are so overwhelming in their implications, yet almost every decision carries with it an opportunity to use constructive conflict. There are different types of conflict. Distinguish between destructive conflict in groups, which is often personal or politically motivated, and constructive conflict that helps to surface differences of opinion and goals. Harnessing this constructive conflict can lead to better decisions.

> Almost every decision carries with it an opportunity to use constructive conflict.

TRUTH

34

Surround yourself with
people smarter than
yourself

Industrialist Andrew Carnegie once suggested that his epitaph should read, "Here lies a man who was able to surround himself with men far cleverer than himself." While there is some degree of false modesty in this statement, Carnegie built an outstanding team of executives who helped him to build one of the leading steel companies in the U.S. Carnegie Steel was sold to JP Morgan's U.S. Steel in 1901 for $400 million. Carnegie was not a gambling man and said that he never bought a share of stock on margin in his life, but he did place his bets on outstanding colleagues.

Some leaders will surround themselves with yes-men and -women who will make them look good—at least in the short run. But in the long run, the decisions of these leaders will suffer. They will find their own first ideas confirmed by those around them rather than challenged by sharper minds. As Enron's collapse has shown, even "the smartest guys in the room" (to quote the title from the book by Bethany McLean and Peter Elkin on Enron's meltdown) were able to make incredibly foolish decisions that brought down the seventh largest company in the U.S.

Surrounding yourself with people who are not only smarter than you, but smart in different ways, can give you the breadth of perspective needed to make better decisions.

Carnegie's colleagues included Charles M. Schwab, who was a financial wizard, and Henry Frick, who was an iron-fisted operational manager. Frick crushed the bloody Homestead strike in 1892, setting back unionization efforts for decades. A week later, he was shot twice, stabbed, and nearly blown up by a would-be assassin. Frick quietly bound up his wounds and continued working for the rest of the day. He refused to back down. His approach and decisions were in sharp contrast to the more conciliatory Carnegie, but together they were able to build a very successful business.

In making decisions, keep a spirit of humility. Seek out people who are smarter than you. This requires setting aside your ego and concentrating on making the best decisions possible. Don't be afraid to ask the foolish question that can

Keep a spirit of humility.

lead to a better decision. Don't be afraid not to be the expert. Surround yourself with people smarter than yourself, and you will look smarter than you are.

Don't be afraid not to be the expert.

TRUTH

35

Make decision roles clear

President George W. Bush once commented, "I am the decider." You may not have always agreed with his decisions, but this statement made his role very clear. Sometimes when groups come together to make decisions, it isn't clear who is actually going to make the final decision. This leads to finger-pointing and inaction. For making complex group decisions, especially in teams where there is no clear leader, roles need to be clear upfront. The most important roles are who will make the decision, who will need to give input on it, and who will need to implement it. You need to decide how you're going to decide.

First, decide how to manage the decision. I once served on a board of a nonprofit that had an unusual twin governance structure. We made decisions based on a majority vote, but the parallel governing body made decisions based on consensus. This led to some potentially awkward moments when the two bodies disagreed. A consensus process is certainly much slower and can be more contentious, but it might lead to more solidarity once it comes time to implement the plan. A majority decision can be quicker, but it can leave many members of the group feeling left out, so it can be the nucleus of a revolution. The fastest and most direct way is for a single decision maker to gather all the information and decide. But while dictatorship may be the most efficient form of government, it isn't always the best way. The type of decision process used may affect later acceptance and implementation.

> The most important roles are who will make the decision, who will give input on it, and who will implement it.

Bain consultants Paul Rogers and Marcia Blenko note that in complex organizations, decisions can be stuck in four key bottlenecks: global versus local, center versus business unit, function versus function, and inside versus outside partners.[22] At these points, there can be questions about who gets to decide what. The classic question is whether decisions should be made at the top of the company—at corporate where they can be aligned with the overall company vision—or down in the business units that are closer to customers.

You also need to decide who needs to give input to the decision. Who has the knowledge that is needed to make the decision? Who can offer advice and perspectives? The more diverse the group giving input, the more complete a picture the ultimate decision maker (or decision makers) will have.

The more diverse the group giving input, the more complete a picture the ultimate decision maker will have.

Finally, you need to determine who will need to implement the decision. If these implementers are not involved in the process upfront, will they understand it and feel ownership enough to actively make it happen?

TRUTH

Break free from the prisoner's dilemma

You and an accomplice are arrested for robbing a bank and are held in separate cells. You can't talk to one another. You have hidden the loot, so the prosecutor doesn't have enough to put either of you away. He offers each of you an attractive deal: Turn on your accomplice, and you will go free (and be able to grab all the loot for yourself). If you remain silent and your accomplice rats you out, however, you will get ten years. If you both remain silent, however, you will both go free (and split the loot). You can't talk to one another. Should you betray your accomplice?

This is the prisoner's dilemma. If you can't trust your accomplice not to sing, the best course for both of you individually is to betray the other. If you remain mum, you could face ten years if your partner squeals. And this is what he would rationally do. The best outcome for everyone collectively is to keep quiet. But the rational move individually is to betray the other.

We can see this in geopolitics where arms races start because neither side can trust the other to stabilize or reduce its levels of armaments. This dynamic can also be seen in price wars where neither side can trust the other to back down. This leads to escalation that might be rational in the individual analysis but leads to an irrational result overall because everyone is worse off in the long run than if they cooperated.

In the classic game, there is no way for the two sides to break free because they can't communicate with one another. In the real world, there usually are opportunities for the two sides to communicate with one another—as was done in the SALT talks during the Cold War—but only if they can recognize that they face a prisoner's dilemma. Are you in a situation where you're better off cooperating than maximizing your own returns separately? Look for opportunities to cooperate either through direct communication or, if this is not possible (for example, if discussing price may lead to charges of price fixing) through signaling your intention to the other party.

When the dilemma is repeated over several rounds with the same players, those that cooperate do better. Nice guys do finish first. It

Nice guys do finish first.

may mean that enlightened players will choose this course on the first round, assuming their partners are also similarly enlightened. But few prisoners may be willing to stake their lives or freedoms on this.

Look at the bigger picture and find a broader solution that produces the best return for everyone.

When facing a decision involving others, don't just look for the solution that maximizes your own return. Look at the bigger picture and find a broader solution that produces the best return for everyone. And then look for ways to encourage cooperation. This may be the best way to break out of prison and create a better solution.

TRUTH

37

A little adrenaline can be a good thing

Samuel Johnson once said, "When a man knows he is to be hanged in a fortnight, it concentrates his mind wonderfully." This can be true, particularly in critical, time-sensitive decisions. The adrenaline rush of the fight-or-flight response has kept human beings out of the jaws of saber-tooth tigers or allowed jet fighter pilots to pull out of a crash. Stress can lead to improved performance.

Decision making can improve under stress up to a point. It sharpens the mind and keeps us focused. But past that point, stress becomes counterproductive and leads to poor decisions. It results in an "inverted U," where the benefits of stress level off and then go negative. We can see an analogy to physical stress in athletic performance. An athlete who is pushed with a moderate amount of stress will achieve higher levels of performance. But too much stress will lead to injuries and burnout. Performance will suffer.

Stress can lead to a tendency to oversimplify decision making. It can lead to working memory loss and narrow focus. It can lead to a limiting of options and premature closure of alternatives. When time pressure is high, for example, decision makers tend to make a decision without generating or evaluating all the possible alternatives.[23] One research study asked 40 subjects to spend five hours engaged in a forest fire fighting game on the computer. Half had to operate with the added stress of a loud noise, while the others had quiet. The ones with the added stress took a more streamlined approach to decision making, while those with less stress used more in-depth analysis.[24] Another study asked student subjects to evaluate the attractiveness of a set of student apartments based on characteristics such as size and traveling time to the university. As time pressure increased, they tended to give more negative weight to one factor—traveling time—rather than weighing all the alternatives.

Of course, a narrow focus can be a good thing if you're in a real emergency. It might allow you to focus on what is really important as your jet is careening out of control. But pay attention to the impact of stress on your decisions. If the decision is not time critical—you're

Pay attention to the impact of stress on your decisions.

facing a loaded gun or have to make a buy or sell decision on a stock at this instant—then take a moment to diffuse the stress if it is hampering your ability to make a decision. Take action to prevent panic and calm your mind. Take a deep breath, go for a walk, or otherwise break the cycle of panic, slow your heartbeat, and settle your mind. A little stress can be a good thing, but too much can interfere with your decision making.

38

Understand the impact of emotions

A manager is faced with a decision about downsizing the workforce. Two staff positions need to be cut from a pool of ten employees. The ten employees have different lengths of tenure in the organization, different levels of performance, different pay, and different family situations. The employee with the poorest performance, for example, is also one of the longest-term employees and is a single mother with three children. While the manager may not explicitly consider this family situation in making the decision, the negative emotion of firing the single mother may affect the decision outcome.[25] Emotions affect how we make trade-offs in our decisions.

Unless you're Dr. Spock from *Star Trek*, you can't avoid bringing emotions to the table when you're making a decision. The trick is to understand the impact of emotions and manage this impact in making decisions. Emotions tend to make us work harder on a decision, but not necessarily smarter, according to researchers Mary Frances Luce, John W. Payne, and James R. Bettman. Decision makers put more effort into the decision but don't necessarily consider more alternatives and make a better decision. In fact, they may ignore alternatives or avoid making explicit trade-offs to cope with the negative emotions.

> Emotions affect how we make trade-offs in our decisions.

We need to recognize the impact of emotions on our decisions. Once we recognize the potential for negative emotions, we might approach the decision in a way that shields us from the impact of those emotions. We might consider the downsizing decision by making the overall health of the company paramount above the impact on an individual employee. We also might develop a plan for support and transition for employees who are let go, decreasing the perceived personal impact of the decision.

On the other hand, we don't always want to set our emotions aside in making decisions. We sometimes need to find a balance between heart and head. Sometimes emotions can lead us to a decision that we might not have considered otherwise. It might be argued that we won't make a good decision if we don't include emotion. We just need to be aware of emotions, particularly negative ones, and avoid letting them cloud our judgment in making a decision. When we're approaching a decision, we need to look for potentially negative emotions that might be involved. Then we need to develop strategies for addressing them. We also need to be vigilant for decisions that are designed to help avoid confronting these difficult emotions.

Avoid letting them cloud our judgment in making a decision.

TRUTH

Beware of the attractive new shortcut

In April 1846, a group of just over 30 people led by George Donner set out for California from Springfield, Illinois. They picked up other members along the way who wanted to join Donner in taking a new route, "The Hastings Cutoff," through the mountains. The "shortcut" took three weeks longer than the standard route and left them trapped in the blizzards of Sierra Nevada. Nearly half of the 87 pioneers died. The survivors of the Donner party ran short of food, finally forcing some of them to resort to cannibalism.

Sometimes in making decisions, we're faced with a new but untried solution—a shortcut. Take a careful look at the risks involved. Even if the route is less expensive or less time consuming, it could extract a higher cost in the long run. Remember that the untried path carries with it higher costs of breaking new trails and greater risks in venturing into the unknown.

We might not look at the dangers for a couple of reasons. First, we're enamored with the beauty of the solution and the power of our own ideas. If it is a new and different solution, we may look at it like a firstborn child rather than give it a more critical appraisal. Second, in evaluating a new route where there is little experience, we may tend to focus on the upside. Since we haven't lived through the failures and difficulties of this approach, we may give them less weight than they should have. The added costs and risks of an untried path might be justified, but we need to understand what they are.

> Even if the route is less expensive or less time consuming, it could extract a higher cost in the long run.

In making decisions, we may be faced with what looks like an attractive shortcut. Maybe it is an opportunity to bend the rules. Maybe it is cutting corners in a way that is efficient but adds to danger. In considering such options, we will typically look at the positive gains and underestimate the negatives.

A new or different solution can be a great leap forward. It can be a true shortcut that can improve every future decision. This is particularly important where similar decisions are made repeatedly. But this was not the case with the Donner party when they just needed to make it through the mountains one time. Be bold about trying new routes, but also be careful. Examine the potential pitfalls, including the costs and risks added by lost time. Look closely at what could go wrong, before you're trapped in the mountains without food. In the case of the Donner party, the well-trod path might have been a better choice in retrospect. If it still makes sense to proceed, move forward, but be alert for changes in your environment that might signal the need for a different approach.

The added costs and risks of an untried path might be justified, but we need to understand what they are.

TRUTH

40

Don't do anything you wouldn't want seen on YouTube

It used to be that the standard of behavior was not to do anything you didn't want to find on the front page of *The New York Times*. Our modern world offers many more ways to embarrass ourselves, so we no longer have to wait for the morning papers.

Martha Stewart can teach you about a lot more than a good place setting. The small decisions that we make along the way and the values that guide those decisions can have significant impact. Stewart thought she received a quiet call from an old friend about an investment and then made a personal decision about selling shares. But the old friend was the CEO who had inside information about a pending rejection of a key drug by the FDA. It was a simple and relatively small decision compared to many large ones in the vast empire that Martha Stewart controlled. But this decision took over her life, sent her into court and to jail, and tarnished her reputation. Suddenly a private decision became front-page news. Don't do anything you wouldn't want your parents to see on the evening news.

Alfred Nobel had the rare experience of reading his own obituary while he was still alive. In 1888, when his brother Ludvig died, a French newspaper mistakenly ran an obituary for Alfred. Imagine his surprise when he picked up the paper and read the headline on the obituary: "The merchant of death is dead."

Referring to Nobel's invention of dynamite, the obituary said that the inventor of the most powerful and destructive force known to man had died. Nobel didn't like the look of that, so he made the decision to rewrite his will.

When Nobel actually died in 1896, his relatives were shocked to learn that most of his considerable fortune would go to establish the Nobel prizes. Now, Nobel is best remembered for recognizing and supporting excellence in diverse fields from physics to world peace.

What decisions could you make today that would rewrite your history?

An interesting exercise to engage in periodically is to write your own obituary. What would your obituary say if it were written today? What would you like it to say? What decisions could you make today that would rewrite your history?

TRUTH

41

There are no quiet corners
safe from scrutiny

Umberto Nobile was a brilliant engineer and aviator, but his career was ruined in part by a split-second decision he made on the Arctic ice. In 1928, his airship *Italia* crashed on the ice during a North Pole flight. He lost part of his crew, and the rest were stranded in a little, red tent as the world mobilized a massive rescue effort. After many days on the ice, a small French plane managed to land. The pilot insisted that Nobile himself should be the first to leave with him. Nobile finally gave in. Then he could help to guide the rescue parties back to the others. Nobile left with his lapdog, leaving his men behind. This violated every principle of the captain going down with the ship, and this was how it looked to the world when he returned. Whatever actually happened on the ice, the world remembers only that the captain and his pooch took off before his men.

It's hard to think of a more remote location for making a decision than on a barren piece of polar ice. But the decision was broadcast to the world. And no one remembered anything else—just that Nobile had saved himself and his dog before his men. Nobile returned to Italy in disgrace. Despite his spectacular successes in engineering, aviation, and exploration, a split-second decision, literally in the middle of nowhere, ultimately defined how Nobile's career was viewed. And that was back when news traveled by telegraph.

Face it. We live in an increasingly interconnected world, even more so than Nobile. What you do today in the confines of your own home could end up known to the world tomorrow. If you're a policeman who thinks you can make a decision to beat up an obstreperous arrestee on a back street (as in the case of Rodney King), you could find yourself on national television. If your sneakers or toys are made by children in a sweatshop in rural Asia, remember that no matter how remote this might seem, all will eventually be revealed.

We live in an increasingly interconnected world.

The decision of major global drug companies to sue African companies over patent infringements might have seemed like a good idea in a mahogany tabled conference room in the U.S. After all, the foundation of innovation is patent protection, and without it there will be little incentive for pioneers to innovate. But once the decision hit the newsstands, the picture was quite different. In a global context, this was a group of greedy multinationals putting the screws on poor, Third World countries with serious health problems. The drug companies were quickly forced to rethink their decisions. But if they had given more attention to how their decisions would be viewed, they might have avoided a lot of bad ink.

For decisions that are made in backrooms, over dinner, or on a remote stretch of ice, take a moment to shine the light on them. What would happen if these decisions were broadcast to the world? Would you be comfortable opening the kimono, or do you have something to hide? Of course, you can do your best to make sure that your decisions are not broadcast to the world (check for cameras), but in

What would happen if these decisions were broadcast to the world?

a world where information is fluid, if the decision is at all important, it is more likely than ever to see the light of day. So when you're making any decision, particularly a private one, always consider how it might play on the public stage.

TRUTH

42

To know where you're going, know where you stand

The shareholder view is that the role of the firm is to maximize profits for shareholders. It isn't the firm's role to be concerned about its broader human, social, or political impact except to the extent that it generates greater return for shareholders. The stakeholder view of the firm holds that the company must take into account the interests of other stakeholders, including customers, community members in areas in which it operates, employees, and other players who are affected by the firm's actions. In the most optimistic view, these perspectives come together in the idea that while the shareholder view maximizes returns for the short run, the stakeholder view maximizes returns for the long run by adding value to intangible assets such as brand and reputation. The stakeholder view creates a sustainable enterprise. This belief is embodied in the Johnson & Johnson "Credo," which states that if the company meets the needs of patients, customers, employees, and other stakeholders, investors will be rewarded.

The stakeholder view led Merck to create a drug for river blindness or Glaxo SmithKline to create a drug for meningitis that is marketed only in Africa. There may not have been a profitable market for these drugs, but they were the right thing to do. The first priority was not shareholders, but rather addressing devastating illnesses in Africa.

In your personal career, one view is that advancement is based on a Darwinian, dog-eat-dog struggle for survival and maximizing personal wealth (the Gordon Gecko or Enron view). This is in contrast to the view of maximizing the contributions of your career to your organization and the world. These different views will lead to very different sets of decisions about your career and within your career.

The decisions you make depend on your moral compass, on where you are starting from. Some of the most important decisions can't be weighed only in the head but also need to be weighed in the heart. Is it the right thing to do? Is the decision

> Some of the most important decisions can't be weighed only in the head but also need to be weighed in the heart.

consistent with your convictions or does it go against your deepest beliefs?

What are the core religious or personal beliefs that underlie your decision making?

Look into your heart. Where do you start from in making decisions? What are the core religious or personal beliefs that underlie your decision making? How do you need to decide to remain true to these beliefs? What are alternative views that you might adopt? How do these different views lead to decisions and actions?

TRUTH

43

Don't let power or ego sway you from your course

It's easy to make ethical decisions in a vacuum. In a hypothetical world, we would never bend the rules or cheat. But what if the second-most powerful man in America asks you to do something that doesn't sit right? How do you say no?

This was the challenge faced by billionaire industrialist Jon Huntsman as a member of the Nixon White House. Nixon's Chief of Staff H. R. Haldeman asked Huntsman to send someone from his company to spy on a political rival. Huntsman got as far as picking up the phone and calling one of his managers, but he caught himself in time. It was the beginning of the end of Huntsman's career in the Nixon White House, but he was virtually the only top staff member of the Nixon administration who was not indicted in the Watergate scandal.[26]

In a famous set of experiments by Yale University psychologist Stanley Milgram, participants were told by an authority figure to administer shocks to another "subject" (actually an actor) in a different room. As an authority figure in a white lab coat supervised, the actors were given a series of questions. If the actors gave the wrong answer, subjects were instructed to give them an electric shock, starting at 45 volts and increasing with every wrong answer. The subjects believed they were giving actual shocks to the actors. As the voltages rose, the actors screamed and banged on the wall. The observer in the white lab coat reassured the subjects and urged them to go on. In the experiments, no subject stopped the shocks before 300 volts, and more than three-fifths the subjects administered the maximum (450 volts). We have a tremendous need to conform, particularly to the orders of an authority figure.

The experiments, begun in 1961, shortly after the trial of Nazi war criminal Adolf Eichmann, were designed to explore how ordinary people might have engaged in the extraordinary atrocities of the Holocaust. The chilling results showed how susceptible we all are to the power of authority and the

> If we find ourselves pushed into a decision that makes us feel uncomfortable, we need to be willing to question authority.

need for compliance in making our decisions. If we find ourselves pushed into a decision that makes us feel uncomfortable, we need to be willing to question authority.

One small compromise can lead to bigger ones. It's a slippery slope. Financier Larry Zicklin of Neuberger & Berman said compromising ethics is like the "salami theory." You keep slicing off a little bit of your ethics, and pretty soon there's nothing left.

When you're making an important decision, consider the pressure that is placed on you to decide in a certain way. The pressure could be from a boss or other important manager, or it could be from family, a doctor, or another authority figure. Remember that these authority figures may fall from their pedestal in the future. Would you still be comfortable with your decision if this happened? These influencers may place undue pressure to decide in a certain way. You need to check with your own values. You wouldn't be human if you weren't influenced by others,

> Would you make the same decision if it were yours alone to make?

but you need to make sure you're not swayed too much by those around you. Would you make the same decision if it were yours alone to make?

TRUTH

Lower the costs of failure

In building Standard Oil, John D. Rockefeller collaborated with the railroads to come up with a system of drawbacks. He paid only 10 cents a barrel to ship his oil, while competitors paid 35 cents. Rockefeller received a drawback on the shipping of competitors' products, so he made money every time rivals shipped. Even when he lost, he won.

This made it nearly impossible for other companies to compete. They were forced to sell out to Rockefeller or be driven out of business. (One of Rockefeller's own brothers resisted and was crushed. Another brother complied and became a multimillionaire.) Standard Oil gained 95 percent of U.S. oil production. While this became a classic example of iron-handed anticompetitive monopolies that led to the creation of the Sherman Antitrust Act and the breakup of Rockefeller's Standard Oil, it also represents a diabolically clever decision that helped build one of the greatest American fortunes. Rockefeller was able to design a system that allowed him to win no matter what. This, of course, gives a new and more sinister meaning to the concept of a win-win solution.

Such a solution usually isn't possible or desirable ethically, but even if we can't actually benefit from failure, we can look for opportunities to lower the cost of failure in a big decision. The choice of a job or a spouse is a decision that will affect the rest of your life. The cost of failure makes experimentation difficult. But we can often change the framing of the decision to lower the risks and costs of experimenting. Sometimes we can break down big decisions that appear absolute into smaller experiments that allow us to learn. Instead of taking a new job in a new area, we can start with a hobby in that area and test the waters.

Sam Walton, who began work as an associate at JC Penney earning $75 per week and ended up creating the most successful retail enterprise in history, was legendary for his parsimony. He drove a beat-up pickup truck. He traveled around his expanding empire using a secondhand plane and stayed at

> Sometimes we can break down big decisions that appear absolute into smaller experiments that allow us to learn.

budget motels. Having flirted with disaster throughout the early years of his retail operations, he knew the value of running a lean operation. This lowered his costs of failure.

In making decisions, look for ways to keep the costs down to lower the risks of failure and give yourself more margin for success. This is particularly important for big decisions where the costs of failure can be very high. If you can't find a way to profit from failure, as Rockefeller did, at least limit the pain.

> In making decisions, look for ways to keep the costs down to lower the risks of failure and give yourself more margin for success.

TRUTH

45

Break down big decisions into smaller ones

In 1803, President Thomas Jefferson commissioned Meriwether Lewis and William Clark to lead an expedition to the Pacific Ocean. They would initially follow the Missouri and Columbia Rivers, across the Rocky Mountains, to see if they could find a water route to the west. Their Corps of Discovery covered 8,000 miles in just over two years. While they failed to find a route entirely by water, they charted the geography and learned about the wildlife and native people, opening the West to later exploration and settlement.

While they had a general plan for heading west to the Pacific, starting on the Missouri River and moving to the Columbia, the explorers made their way one campsite at a time. When they heard the thunder of waterfalls, they portaged. When they reached a fork in the Missouri, they had to decide which direction to take. When they ran out of water, they went overland across the Rockies. Some of their most important help came from Sacagawea, a Shoshoni tribeswoman who was a native of the Rocky Mountain region, whom they didn't meet until they reached what is now South Dakota. Jefferson acknowledged that not only the route was uncertain, but also their reception by the peoples of the West. "As it is impossible for us to foresee in what manner you will be received by those people, whether with hospitality or hostility, so is it impossible to prescribe the exact degree of perseverance with which you are to pursue your journey."[27]

The decisions involved in such an expedition could have been overwhelming, but they were made step by step. Large, long-term decisions can be broken down into a series of smaller steps by taking them one day at a time or by establishing interim milestones. For example, in launching a new business based on a new product, the first step might be to gain seed funding from a venture capital fund or angel investor. The next milestone might be to create a product prototype and do market testing. The next step would be to do a

Large, long-term decisions can be broken down into a series of smaller steps by taking them one day at a time or by establishing interim milestones.

broader rollout and then, assuming success, move into a full-scale business. The final step might be a sale or IPO, or a decision to continue to build the business. If you want to buy a car, the first step might be to decide your price range and research the options. Then you might decide on the type of car you want to buy: a family van, station wagon, or sedan. Are your goals better gas mileage, styling, or lower repair bills? You might then test drive a few candidates and discuss financing. Finally, you could make the purchase. By focusing on each smaller goal, you make your way one step at a time toward a larger goal.

> By focusing on each smaller goal, you make your way one step at a time toward a larger goal.

If a decision seems so large as to be overwhelming, look at ways you can break it into smaller pieces. What can you reasonably accomplish in a day or a week, and how can you design a small decision before the sun goes down that advances your overall decision process? If you don't have "undaunted courage" (to borrow the title of Stephen Ambrose's famous story of the Lewis and Clark expedition), this approach can make an intimidating decision a little less daunting.

TRUTH

46

Don't forget the screwdrivers

In making big decisions, don't forget to pay attention to the small details. In the Battle of Isandlwana (in what is currently South Africa) in January 1879, British troops were almost completely annihilated by Zulu warriors armed primarily with spears. The British had modern weapons and crates of ammo, but they had failed to bring enough screwdrivers. While they tried desperately to open the ammo boxes with stones and bayonets, the Zulus stormed their positions and defeated them.

While subsequent analysis of the battle raised other reasons that contributed to the failure, the point of the story is clear: Small details matter. All the best equipment and best training in the world—all the military strategy and decisions—were for naught because of the lack of a few screwdrivers to open the ammo boxes.

While a good strategy is essential, execution can make or break the strategy. At this point, you really do need to sweat the small stuff. A great battlefield plan depends on every unit showing up where it's supposed to be at the right time. A good business strategy depends on everyone recognizing and executing his responsibilities.

> While a good strategy is essential, execution can make or break the strategy.

In executing business strategies, Larry Bossidy, former CEO of Honeywell International, Inc., and Ram Charan, world-renowned consultant and author, emphasize that success depends on the right behaviors, a culture that rewards execution, and a system for having the right people in the right jobs. Bossidy describes a generator developed by Honeywell that could have been a promising entry for supplying backup power for small businesses. The decision to produce this product was a good one. It was an attractive market. But the product was all wrong. It was too small for the target market and ran only on natural gas, while customers were looking for generators that could use both gas and oil. It was too late to fix the mistake, and Bossidy was forced to shut the business down. It was a great idea that failed in its execution.[28]

We spend a lot of time getting the big picture for our decisions right. We agonize over strategic decisions, but it is the small operational and executional issues that can undermine the outcome of the best decisions. While planning for the big picture, don't forget the screwdrivers.

It is the small operational and executional issues that can undermine the outcome of the best decisions.

TRUTH

47

Keep your eye on the long term

Sometimes what looks like a bad decision turns out to be a good one. There is an old Taoist story about a farmer who loses one of his prize horses. His neighbor shakes his head and offers his condolences. The farmer replies, "Who knows what is good or bad?"

The next day, the horse returns, bringing several wild horses with it. Looking at the full pen, the neighbor congratulates the farmer on his good fortune. The farmer says, "Who knows what is good or bad?"

The next day one of the wild horses kicks the farmer's son, breaking his leg. The neighbor shakes his head about the farmer's bad luck. But the farmer replies again, "Who knows what is good or bad?"

The following day, soldiers come to find conscripts for the army. But because the son has a broken leg, he is passed over. The neighbor again congratulates the farmer on his good luck.

And so the story goes. Every decision that looks bad at first turns out to be good in the long run.

The message is to have some equanimity and perspective about decision making. Don't get too caught up in the short-term outcome because the long-term one could be quite different. Enron's Jeff Skilling seemed to be making great decisions right up to the point when the company self-destructed and he ended up on trial.

There are two problems we need to confront. First, we get too caught up in the short-term outcomes of decisions. We fail to see that they might play out differently in the long run. We need to keep our eye on the long term. You may have missed that last turn on the highway, but you will still get to the meeting on time. And even if you're late, it might turn out for the best. Perhaps you will miss the serious accident you would have hit a few moments before. When you lose a job that you hate, it might open the possibility to find one that you love. It is impossible to plan for such contingencies, of course, and they usually

> Don't get too caught up in the short-term outcome because the long-term one could be quite different.

can't be factored into decisions ahead of time. But after you make a decision, keep a healthy, long-term perspective on the results.

Second, we tend to consider only one possible outcome—like the farmer's neighbor—rather than considering all the possible outcomes. Some people will always assume the worst. If you're one of these pessimists, try to force yourself to look at the best possible outcome from a decision. Others always assume things will work out for the best. If you're one of these optimists, try to consider what might go wrong. If we can avoid being blinded by what we expect to happen as a result of a decision, we can do a better job of making one.

If we can avoid being blinded by what we expect to happen as a result of a decision, we can do a better job of making one.

So the next time your horse runs away, remember that it might just keep your son from being conscripted, no matter what your neighbor says.

TRUTH

48

Belief in your decision can make it come true

Cyrus McCormick had lost everything except the mechanical reaper he had invented. In the panic of 1837, he went bankrupt. The bank took his house, his farm, everything—except his reaper. Like the rest of the world, the bank considered it worthless. It wasn't even worth repossessing. McCormick was the only one who believed it was the future of agriculture. He continued to build and sell his reapers, but it was slow going. By 1844, he had sold 50. If he had walked away then, he'd have been considered a failure. But he didn't. He offered demonstrations that showed how the machines outperformed manual labor. He gave money-back guarantees and payment options to make the reapers more affordable. And they finally took off. By the time McCormick died in 1884, he was the richest man in Illinois, with a fortune of at least $10 million. (Some estimates placed it as high as $100 million.) He had built a business that became the foundation of International Harvester— all from his "worthless" reaper.

McCormick's success was based in part on his marvelous machine that finally transformed agriculture forever. But his success was also based on his perseverance in pursuing a decision that most people couldn't see any sense in. Many people would have quit and tried something different, and the decision to pursue a mechanical reaper would then have been considered failure. McCormick took more than a decade of failure and ultimately turned it into a success. We can't underestimate the power of passion or sheer chutzpah in making a decision successful.

We see this same bizarre confidence in the decision by Col. Joshua Chamberlain during the U.S. Civil War battle at Gettysburg. Chamberlain was charged with holding the critical Union position at Little Round Top against a Confederate attack. In a fierce battle with enemy troops, Chamberlain's men finally had enough ammunition for just one more volley. Yet the enemy pressed forward. Chamberlain ordered his men to load their weapons, fix their bayonets, and charge the enemy. The shocked Confederates turned and fled. This gutsy move may have saved the battle by protecting the Union flank.

Once you make a decision, believe in it. It is often the belief in an outcome that makes the

Once you make a decision, believe in it.

outcome come true. Our minds are more powerful than we think. In one study, nearly a third of a group of chemotherapy patients lost their hair. This may not seem surprising, perhaps, but these patients were in the group that was given a placebo, not the actual drug. They lost their hair because they expected to lose their hair. This is the placebo effect. Our thinking and expectations do not control everything around us, but they do have much more of an impact than we realize.

When you commit to a decision, commit wholeheartedly. This passion and confidence could make what is essentially a bad decision turn out for the best. Sometimes a bad decision can become a good one through the sheer force of will. As William James wrote, "Often enough our faith beforehand in an uncertified result is the only thing that makes the result come true."

> Our thinking and expectations do not control everything around us, but they do have much more of an impact than we realize.

TRUTH

Keep a sense of humor

Some older kids were in the habit of offering a young and gullible sibling the choice between a nickel and a dime. Every time the kids did this, the younger sibling chose the nickel, "because it's bigger."

One day, a friend took the poor kid aside and asked, "Don't you know that a dime's worth more than a nickel?"

The kid answered, "Yeah, but if I picked the dime they'd stop doing it!"[29]

Decisions can be complex and stressful, but always try to approach decision making with a healthy sense of humor. If you take your decisions too seriously, you may tend to overanalyze and procrastinate, which could erode your ability to make a good decision.

Don't let the magnitude of the decision overwhelm you. Sure, a decision can affect the rest of your life—it might even be a life or death decision—but you will make better decisions if you keep a sense of perspective and humor about it. As Oscar Wilde once said, "Life is too important to be taken seriously."

If you take your decisions too seriously, you may tend to overanalyze and procrastinate.

Try to find some humor—even if it is dark humor—in every situation you face. If you can't manage a belly laugh, at least look at the problem and smile. Doing that will change the way you look at the problem. And it might open your mind to some new perspectives.

And be sure to include some humorous options when you consider what to do. These can push the limits of your thinking and may lead to some good ideas in the end. For example, when a manufacturer who used newspapers to pack products was brainstorming about a way to keep employees from reading the papers, slowing productivity, one manager suggested in jest to poke their eyes out. It clearly was not a solution that could be pursued. But the tongue-in-cheek suggestion resulted in a discussion that led to a more practical approach: using foreign newspapers that the employees couldn't read.

By the way, the kid in the opening story actually used humor to influence the decisions of others. This is another use of humor in decision making. This boy wasn't afraid to be the butt of the joke as long as the nickels kept flowing. He may not have made a rational decision on the surface, but he was certainly laughing all the way to the bank.

TRUTH

50

Don't look back

You can live life in only one direction. Once you make a decision, look back only long enough to learn from it. Then look forward, because there will be another decision right around the corner. If you're driving using the rearview mirror, you will not see what is coming at you on the road ahead.

You will be tempted to agonize about the decisions gone wrong or to gloat over the ones gone right. The first impulse will blind you with regret. The second will blind you with arrogance. Neither form of blindness will improve your decisions going forward. You need to move ahead with both eyes open.

Learn to forgive and be forgiven. One of the hardest and most important challenges is found in the deceptively simple words of the Lord's Prayer, "Forgive us our trespasses as we forgive those who trespass against us." You will make mistakes. You don't have to forget.

Learn to forgive and be forgiven.

With any luck, you will remember and learn from them. But you do need to forgive, to let go so that you can focus on challenges ahead that are just as serious.

Author Stephen Levine, after working with patients at their deathbeds for many years, conducted a thought experiment in his own life that he chronicles in his book *A Year to Live*.[30] What if you had only one year left to live? How would this change the way you live your life? What decisions would you make? Levine's book is a fascinating exercise that will give you a healthy perspective on life and keep you firmly focused on the road immediately ahead of you.

Make the best decision you can and then get on with it. Say your mea culpas, if necessary. Admit, as politicians are fond of doing, that "mistakes were made." Perhaps you might even be bold enough to admit

Make the best decision you can and then get on with it.

that you made them. Then forge ahead. Your career and life going forward will not be shaped as much by the decisions of your past, as important as they are, as by the ones you're still to make in the future.

182

Additional Resources

Gladwell, Malcolm. *Blink: The Power of Thinking Without Thinking.* New York: Little, Brown and Company, 2005.

Groopman, Jermone. *How Doctors Think.* New York: Houghton Mifflin, 2007.

Hammond, John A., Ralph A. Keeney, and Howard Raiffa. *Smart Choices.* New York: Broadway Books, 1999.

Kunreuther, Howard, and Stephen Hoch, eds., with Robert E. Gunther. *Wharton on Making Decisions.* New York: John Wiley & Sons, 2001.

Robbins, Stephen P. *Decide and Conquer.* New York: Financial Times Prentice Hall, 2004.

Russo, J. Edward, and Paul J. H. Schoemaker. *Decision Traps: The Ten Barriers to Brilliant Decision-Making and How to Overcome Them.* New York: Simon & Schuster, 1990.

Russo, J. Edward, and Paul J. H. Schoemaker. *Winning Decisions.* New York: Currency Doubleday, 2001.

Schoemaker, Paul J. H., and Robert E. Gunther. "The Wisdom of Deliberate Mistakes." *Harvard Business Review* (June 2006): 108–115.

Useem, Michael. *The Go Point: When It's Time to Decide—Knowing What to Do and When to Do It.* New York: Crown Business, 2006.

References

Introduction

1   Kay Redfield Jamison has a delightful description of Roosevelt and other "exuberant" decision makers such as "Snowflake" Bentley (whose passion for photographing snowflakes made him one of the foremost authorities on the topic) in her book *Exuberance: The Passion for Life.* New York: Alfred A. Knopf (Random House), 2004.

2   Gladwell, Malcolm. *Blink: The Power of Thinking Without Thinking.* Little Brown, 2005.

3   LeGault, Michael R. *Th!nk: Why Crucial Decisions Can't Be Made in the Blink of an Eye.* New York: Threshold Editions, 2006.

Truth 2

4   Kopeikina, Luda. *The Right Decision Every Time: How to Reach Perfect Clarity on Tough Decisions.* Upper Saddle River, New Jersey: Prentice Hall, 2005.

Truth 9

5   Phimister, James, Ulku Oktem, Howard Kunreuther, and Paul R. Kleindorfer. "Near-Miss Management Systems in the Chemical Process Industry." *Risk Analysis*, June 2003.

6   Ibid.

Truth 14

7   Johnson, Eric J., John Hershey, Jacqueline Meszaros and Howard Kunreuther, "Framing, probability distortions, and insurance decisions," *Journal of Risk and Uncertainty*, August 1993, 7.1: 35–51.

Truth 15

8   Simons, Daniel J., and Christopher F. Chabris. "Gorillas in Our Midst: Sustained Inattention Blindness for Dynamic Events." *Perception* 28 (1999): 1059–1074.

For further discussion of the implications of this study, see Yoram (Jerry) Wind and Colin Crook, *The Power of Impossible Thinking,*

Upper Saddle River, NJ: Wharton School Publishing, 2005; and George S. Day and Paul J.H. Schoemaker, *Peripheral Vision,* Boston: Harvard Business School Press, 2006, p. 21,

Truth 16

9 Groopman, Jerome. "What's the Trouble? How Doctors Think." *The New Yorker* (January 29, 2007): 36–41.

Truth 18

10 Gause, Donald C., and Gerald M. Weinberg. *Are Your Lights On?: How to Figure Out What the Problem Really Is,* New York: Dorset House Publishing Company, 1990.

Truth 20

11 Kahn, Barbara, and Andrea Morales. "Choosing Variety." in *Wharton on Making Decisions.* Kunreuther, Howard, and Stephen Hoch, eds., New York: John Wiley & Sons, 2001, 63–80.

Truth 21

12 Pollan, Michael. "Unhappy Meals." *The New York Times Magazine* (January 28, 2007): 39.

13 Meyer, Robert J., and J. Wesley Hutchinson. "Bumbling Geniuses: The Power of Everyday Reasoning in Multistage Decision Making." in *Wharton on Making Decisions.* Kunreuther, Howard, and Stephen Hoch, eds., New York: John Wiley & Sons, 2001, 37–61.

Truth 23

14 Thomson, Clive. "Bicycle Helmets Put You at Risk." *The New York Times Magazine,* December 10, 2006: 36.

Truth 25

15 www.Iraqbodycount.com.

Truth 26

16 Carey, John. "Medical Guesswork," *BusinessWeek,* May 29, 2006, p. 72.

Truth 31

17 Drucker, Peter F., *Management: Tasks, Responsibilities and Practices,* New York: Harper & Row, 1974: 475–476.

Truth 32

18 The term is attributed to William Whyte in a *Fortune* article in 1952, although the phenomenon was explored in more detail by Irving Janis in his book *Victims of Groupthink*. Boston: Houghton Mifflin Company, 1972.

Truth 33

19 Kennedy, Robert F. *Thirteen Days: A Memoir of the Cuban Missile Crisis*. New York: WW Norton & Company (1969): 44.

20 Surowiecki, James. *The Wisdom of Crowds: Why the Many Are Smarter Than the Few and How Collective Wisdom Shapes Business, Economies, Societies and Nations*. New York: Doubleday, 2004.

21 Ibid., 3.

Truth 35

22 Rogers, Paul, and Marcia Blenko. "Who Has the D? How Clear Decision Roles Enhance Organizational Performance." *Harvard Business Review* (January 2006).

Truth 37

23 *Maule, A. J. and O. Svenson. Time Pressure and Stress in Human Judgment and Decision Making. New York: Plenum Press, 1993.*

24 Kowalski-Trakofler, K. M., C. Vaught, and T. Scharf. "Judgment and Decision Making Under Stress: An Overview for Emergency Managers." *International Journal of Emergency Management*, Vol. 1, No. 3 (2003): 278–289.

Truth 38

25 Luce, Mary Frances, John W. Payne, and James R. Bettman. "The Emotional Nature of Decision Trade-Offs." *Wharton on Making Decisions*. Kunreuther, Howard, and Stephen Hoch, eds., New York: John Wiley & Sons, 2001, 17-35.

Truth 43

26 Huntsman, Jon. *Winners Never Cheat: Everyday Values We Learned as Children (But May Have Forgotten)*. Upper Saddle River, New Jersey: Wharton School Publishing, 2005.

Truth 45

27 www.monticello.org/jefferson/lewisandclark/instructions.html.

Truth 46

28 Bossidy, Larry, and Ram Charan. *Execution: The Discipline of Getting Things Done.* New York: Crown Business (2002): 3–4.

Truth 49

29 Baron, Jonathan. "Psychology Humor." Attributed to Barry F. Anderson, http://www.psych.upenn.edu/humor.html.

Truth 50

30 Levine, Stephen. *A Year to Live: How to Live This Year as if It Were Your Last.* New York: Bell Tower (Random House), 1997.

About the Author

Robert Gunther is coauthor or collaborator on more than 20 books. Among many projects, he served as collaborating writer on *Wharton on Making Decisions* and coauthored *The Wealthy 100*, a ranking of the wealthiest Americans since the start of the country. His books have been translated into more than a dozen languages. He has appeared on CNBC's "Power Lunch," NPR's "Morning Edition," and numerous local and national radio and television programs. His projects also have been featured in *The New York Times, Time, USA Today*, and *Fortune*. His columns or articles have been published in *Harvard Business Review, American Heritage, Investor's Business Daily*, and *The Philadelphia Inquirer*.

As founder of Gunther Communications, he has collaborated with leading business professors on books and articles, and engaged in communications work for Fortune 500 companies, universities, and major non-profits. After graduating from Princeton University, he worked as a reporter and editor for *The Press of Atlantic City*. He later joined the Wharton School where he served as director of development communications and director of publications in executive education. He and his wife have three children and live outside Philadelphia.